NEW YORK GIANTS

75 YEARS OF
FOOTBALL MEMORIES

From the archives of the

DAILY 🔲 NEWS

Published by Sports Publishing Inc.
www.SportsPublishingInc.com

DAILY ◉ NEWS

VICTORIA J. PARRILLO, Coordinating Editor

JOSEPH J. BANNON, JR., Development and Research Editor
SUSAN M. MCKINNEY, Director of Production
TERRY N. HAYDEN, Interior and Dustjacket Design
ERIC MESKAUSKAS AND ANGELA TROISI, Photo Editors
DAVID HAMBURG, Copy editor

ISBN 1-58261-134-3
Library of Congress Catalog Card Number: 99-65758

Published by Sports Publishing Inc.
www.SportsPublishingInc.com

Printed in the United States

Acknowledgments

Throughout the past 75 years of New York Giants football, the *Daily News* has given its readers a front-row seat for every historic moment. Bringing the most memorable events in Giants history to life every day in the pages of the *Daily News* requires the hard work and dedication of hundreds of people at the paper. When we first approached the *Daily News* about this project, we received the overwhelming support of Les Goodstein (Executive Vice President/Associate Publisher) and Ed Fay (VP/Director of Editorial Administration). Among others at the paper who were instrumental in assisting us in this project were Lenore Schlossberg, John Polizano, Eric Meskauskas, Angela Troisi, Mike Lipack, Vincent Panzarino, Faigi Rosenthal, Peter Edelman and Scott Browne. From the *Daily News* sports department, I specifically want to acknowledge the cooperation and support of editor Leon Carter.

Space limitations preclude us from thanking each writer and photographer whose work appears in this book. However, wherever available, we have preserved the writers' bylines and the photographers' credits to ensure proper attribution for their work.

And finally, I am grateful for all the support and hard work of those at Sports Publishing Inc. who worked tirelessly on this project: Joe Bannon, Jr., Susan McKinney, Mike Pearson, Terry Hayden, Jennifer Polson, David Hamburg, Claudia Mitroi, Terrence Miltner, Joanna Wright, Julie Denzer, and Scot Muncaster.

Victoria J. Parrillo
Coordinating Editor

Table of Contents

Introduction

When the American Professional Football League formed a loose association of teams in 1920 and renamed itself the National Football League in 1922, not even the most optimistic observer could have imagined the billion-dollar industry that was being spawned. Certainly not Gotham's Tim Mara, who plunked down $500 in 1925 to purchase the New York Giants franchise. But over the past half century, the NFL has exploded to unbelievable heights and now sits as the king of American sports.

Every step of the way, the growth of professional football has been marked by a significant moment from the 75-year history of the New York Giants:

- When Red Grange first brought the NFL to popular prominence in 1925, his grandest stage was the Polo Grounds against the Giants.
- When pro football stepped in to help combat the economic hardships of the Great Depression, it was the Giants against Knute Rockne's famed Notre Dame squad in a 1930 charity game.
- When the first Pro Bowl was played after the conclusion of the 1938 season, New York's NFL-champion Giants defeated the Pro All-Stars, 13-10.
- When the world went to war in WWII, two Giant players gave their lives, and one of them, Jack Lummus, was awarded the Congressional Medal of Honor for his courageous sacrifice at Iwo Jima.
- When pro football was launched into the living rooms of millions of Americans in the late 1950s and early 1960s, it was the Giants who played in six of the eight championship games during that period, including 1958's "Greatest Game Ever Played."
- When the Giants' star Emlen Tunnell was hired as an assistant coach in 1965 and then inducted into the Pro Football Hall of Fame in 1967, he broke the NFL color barrier on both occasions.
- When the 1970s saw Americans moving to the suburbs, the Giants built one of the first modern football facilities, in New Jersey's Meadowlands.
- When the NFC dominated the Super Bowl with 13 straight victories in the 1980s and '90s, the Giants' Bill Parcells, Lawrence Taylor, and Phil Simms headlined two of the NFC's championship victories.
- When a team finally went through the NFC East undefeated, it was the 1997 New York Giants who accomplished this unparalleled feat.

The Giants' celebrated history is equally evident in the NFL record books, where few teams even approach the success of the New York franchise. The Giants have been involved in more championship games (17, including the 1927 league champions) than any other NFL franchise. And over the past 75 years, the Giants are second only to the Chicago Bears in total games won, with 531 victories, and third on the all-time list of champions, with six NFL titles (1927, 1934, 1938, 1956, 1986, 1990). The Giants also top the list of teams that have finished first in their division most often (19 seasons) and are second in the number of seasons qualifying for the NFL playoffs (24).

NEW YORK GIANTS: 75 YEARS OF FOOTBALL MEMORIES

Beyond the statistics and the records, the history of the New York franchise is populated with great names that instantly bring a smile to the face of any Giant fan. Nearly two dozen of these names have been enshrined in the Pro Football Hall of Fame, and three of them—Lawrence Taylor, Roosevelt Brown, and Mel Hein—were named to the Hall of Fame's 75th Anniversary All-Time NFL Team. Other Giant names—Steve Owen, Ken Strong, Tuffy Leemans, Al Blozis, Frank Gifford, Emlen Tunnell, Del Shofner, and Carl Banks—dominate the Hall of Fame's "Teams of the Decades" selections for the first seven decades of NFL play.

And even this list doesn't include the many other great Giant heroes. For 75 years of Sundays, New Yorkers have also stood and cheered the play of Red Badgro, Ray Flaherty, Eddie Price, Kyle Rote, Tom Landry, Andy Robustelli, Rosey Grier, Sam Huff, Alex Webster, Charlie Conerly, Y.A. Tittle, Jim Katcavage, Fran Tarkenton, Ron Johnson, Phil Simms, Joe Morris, Rodney Hampton, Michael Strahan, and dozens more. The list of Giant stars is a veritable Who's Who of NFL history.

But not every year brought championship glory to the franchise. Like any team in any sport, the Giants have had to endure their lean years, too. Lost championships, unbelievable fumbles, shocking defeats, bad player moves, short-lived coaching stints. They're all part of the Giants' lore. And during these hard times, there's been no shortage of fans to voice their displeasure. But that's the secret of the Giants' 75 years of success—no shortage of fans.

From the 73,000 people who turned out to see the Giants take on Red Grange in 1925 to the 75,000 fans who fill the Meadowlands today, becoming a Giants fan has always been a lifelong commitment—win or lose. Stories abound of season tickets being passed from generation to generation and of the list of 20,000 fans who patiently wait their turn for a season-ticket opening.

Much of the fans' loyalty, of course, reflects the Giants' many triumphs over the past 75 years. But it's more than that. Much more. In many ways, the enduring fan loyalty can be traced to the fact that the Giants themselves have been a family affair ever since the team's founding. The incredible lineage of Mara ownership is recognized by the enshrinement of Tim and Wellington Mara in Pro Football's Hall of Fame—the only father and son so honored.

Whether giving their fans championship thrills or disappointing them with notorious chills and spills, the Giants' remarkable 75-year history is unmatched by any other franchise in professional football. Throughout it all, the *Daily News* has been there, providing New Yorkers with front-row seats for all the Giants' moments. Selecting from among the thousands of great *Daily News* stories and pictures over these past 75 years has been both an exciting challenge and a wonderful adventure.

Looking back through the archives of the Giants' history gives every fan a chance to relive his or her most cherished memories. And for any good fan, it also provides the opportunity to speculate on how many championships the next 75 years will bring.

Sports Publishing Inc.
Joseph J. Bannon, Jr.

MARA PURCHASES PRO FOOTBALL RIGHTS

1925

What started out as a meeting about heavyweight contender Gene Tunney turned out to be the birth of professional football in New York City.

Not too long ago, New York physician Harry March applied for a franchise in the fledgling National Football League. March, an ardent football enthusiast, had been involved with professional football back in his hometown of Canton, Ohio. Thinking that New York needed a team of its own, March set out to raise the $500 franchise fee.

His efforts to secure financing led him to boxing promoter Billy Gibson, who is Gene Tunney's boxing manager. Gibson, who had been talking with (legal) bookmaker Tim Mara about buying an interest in Tunney, suggested that March talk to Mara.

They did, and when Mara learned that the asking price for the new franchise was $500, he promptly dropped his interest in Tunney. Although he has never seen a football game before, Mara told friends that "any franchise in New York is worth that amount of money." After all, the New York Yankees had fetched $460,000 ten years earlier when they were sold to Jacob Ruppert and Colonel Til Huston.

Mara grew up on the Lower East Side, the son of a police officer who died before Mara was born. Mara quit school at 13 to start his career as a bookmaker, eventually setting up shop at Belmont Track. Mara plans to use his winnings from the race track to finance the expected $25,000 that it will cost him to field a team this season.

Mara's new team will be playing its games at the Polo Grounds. Hoping to capitalize on the success of the New York Baseball Giants, Mara has adopted the "Giants" nickname for his new football team.

Mara's football Giants will play their first game on October 11 at the home of the Providence (R.I.) Steam Rollers.

TELLING FRIENDS ABOUT HIS NEWEST SPORTING VENTURE, TIM MARA (LEFT) SAID, RATHER MODESTLY, "I'M GOING TO TRY TO PUT PRO FOOT-BALL OVER IN NEW YORK TODAY." (DAILY NEWS)

25,000 SEE N.Y. GRID
GIANTS LOSE IN HOME OPENER, 14-0

BY JACK FARRELL   OCTOBER 19, 1925

Professional football has come to stay in New York.

At least that was the impression one brought away from the Polo Grounds yesterday. Tim Mara's maiden effort to establish the pro game on Goth's winter sport calendar met with a ready enthusiastic response from the public at large.

Some 25,000 fans saw the New York Giants shut out by the hustling Yellow Jackets from Frankford, Pennsylvania, in a National League game by the score of 14 to 0. Suiting up for the hometown Giants were several players who had earned All-American honors in college, most notably Century Milstead, one of Yale's greatest tackles, and Jim Thorpe, who is the greatest of all football stars.

Against the Yellow Jackets, two touchdowns, one in the first quarter by Johnny Haws, former Dartmouth star, and the other in the second quarter by Tex Hamer, well remembered for his playing at Pennsylvania, proved the undoing of the Giants. Captain Behman kicked both goals.

The visitors out-rushed, outsmarted, out-kicked, and out-gamed the locals in every period with the exception of the third. In that period the Giants launched a heavy air attack which carried them within the shadow of the enemy goal on three different occasions, only to be thwarted by costly fumbles and a stern defense.

The game had all the frills and thrills of a big collegiate game. The Jackets brought along a small army of 5,000 rooters, a set of experienced cheerleaders, and two bands. They paraded around the field between halves and presented a colorful spectacle.

The football Giants now stand at 0 wins and three losses, having dropped their first-ever game at Providence, 14-0, and their earlier matchup with the Yellow Jackets in Frankford, 5-3.

OPPOSITE: TACKLE CENTURY MILSTEAD HELPED THE GIANTS TO A SUCCESSFUL INAUGURAL SEASON. AFTER LOSING THE FIRST THREE GAMES IN THEIR HISTORY, THE GIANTS RE-BOUNDED TO FINISH 8-4 ON THE YEAR. (DAILY NEWS)

70,000 SEE GRANGE'S BEARS WIN, 19-7

Red Intercepts Pass, Runs 35 Yards for Touchdown

BY MARSHALL HUNT   DECEMBER 7, 1925

For three and one-half periods at the humanity-stuffed Polo Grounds yesterday, the metropolitan debut of football's captain of industry was one of the most distinct social and financial successes that New York has ever experienced, but there was something lacking in an artistic way.

Approximately 70,000 pried themselves into the flag-decked, bunting-adorned stadium to see with their own eyes Harold Grange, the very professional ex-student, ex-iceman rip asunder the line of New York's own Giants, to see him wriggle and dart and shimmy his hips for a lengthy run, to see if this famous vendor of ice is all that he is cracked up to be.

They saw, right enough, and during the process, Grange's Chicago Bears defeated the Giants, 19 to 7.

The Giants' winning streak of seven games was wrecked yesterday by Joe Sternaman, who made a touchdown just a few minutes after the game started.

In the same period Grange received a long pass from Larry Walquist, Grange heaved a good pass to Walquist, and this same Joe Sternaman, just a little feller, ran back and across 10 yards for a touchdown.

It was in the second period that Phil White crossed the Bears' line. White and McBride had carried the ball to the 3-yard line and White was designated to score a touchdown. He did, amid much jostling and bucking.

Century Milstead, Lynn Bomar, Mike Palm, Hinkey Haines, Jack McBride, and the other Giants tried their best, but they were up against a formidable set of youths and Harold Grange.

Late into the night, C.C. Pyle, Harold's manager, known as Cash and Carry Pyle, counted up the ex-iceman's earnings on a New York Sabbath. It was rumored that Grange received close to $30,000 for his cut.

A 35-yard run and $30,000.

FINAL EDITION

DAILY NEWS

NEW YORK'S — PICTURE NEWSPAPER

Copyright 1925, by News Syndicate Co. Inc. Reg. U. S. Pat. Off.

Entered as 2nd class matter, Post Office, New York, N. Y.

THE LARGEST CIRCULATION IN AMERICA

Vol. 7. No. 141.   32 Pages   ★★   New York, Monday, December 7, 1925   2 Cents   IN CITY LIMITS | 3 CENTS Elsewhere

70,000 SEE GRANGE STAR

Story on Page 28

Joe Sternaman of the Bears tears through on 30 yard run for a touchdown. Hinkey Haines leaps over interference, but fails to curb Sternaman.

RED'S DEBUT A WOW!—70,000 fans jammed Polo grounds to see Red Grange's professional football debut in New York yesterday and cheered him raucously. He made a touchdown in fourth quarter on 35 yard run, besides numerous other star plays. Chicago Bears defeated Giants, 19 to 7.—*Story on page 28.*

Grange (right, foreground) runs out to take forward pass in second quarter and makes 25 yards on it. Bomar makes powerful leap to intercept pass.

This remarkable football action picture shows Red Grange (arrow) living up to rep at start of game. Note Red getting away for 20 yard end run protected by perfect interference from Giants' tacklers.

Among the peppiest rooters were Mr. and Mrs. Al Smith jr. and their friend Mrs. Joseph Crater (right). They gave Red a big hand, and watched every play like simon pure fans.

Phil White (arrow) was tackled from behind by Grange after running back punt 20 yards in the second quarter. When famous iceman wasn't burning space he was doing effective blocking.

GRID GIANTS TRAP BEARS

BY C.A. LOVETT   NOVEMBER 28, 1927

The New York grid Giants virtually clinched National League pro football titular honors by handing the Chicago Bears a 13-7 beating before 13,500 at the Polo Grounds yesterday. First place was at stake, the Bears being but a game behind the leaders when the clash started. Incidentally, it opened the season series, the Bears having won the odd game of three earlier meetings.

Jack McBride was the outstanding figure in this grim grid struggle, counting both Giant touchdowns in a wild burst of ground spurning in the third quarter after the first half had been scoreless.

Joe Sternaman, Larry Walquist, and Paddy Driscoll collaborated in giving the Bears a touchdown early in the final period, and thereupon Chicago opened up the game, trying for the equalizer. Erratic receiving and a fumble proved costly and the final play was in midfield.

The opening period proved scoreless when Chicago failed to score from the one-yard line.

The second period was a punting due,l with Paddy Driscoll having a slight edge. Neither side seriously threatened to score, and completed passes were rare.

Chicago's line was pierced repeatedly in the second half, and the Giants' parade to the first touchdown was sharp and clean. john Hagerty ran back the kickoff to the N.Y. 45-yard mark, and an overline pass, McBride to Hagerty, netted 15. McBride and Fay Wilson earned three first downs, and the old Syracuse star went over from the two-yard line. He failed to add the point.

The Giants profited largely from another series of punts, and McBride again scored a touchdown, this time from the half-yard mark on a fourth down, and he added the point.

The Bears used a succession of trick plays to score a touchdown early in the fourth, but it wasn't enough.

OPPOSITE: AFTER BEATING THE BEARS AND SWEEPING THE N.Y. FOOTBALL YANKEES TO FINISH THE SEASON WITH A LEAGUE-BEST 11-1-1 RECORD, THE GIANTS WERE DECLARED THE 1927 NFL CHAMPIONS. IT WASN'T UNTIL 1933 THAT THE NFL CHAMPION WAS DETERMINED BY A PLAYOFF.

FINAL EDITION

DAILY NEWS

NEW YORK'S PICTURE NEWSPAPER

THE LARGEST CIRCULATION IN AMERICA

Copyright 1927 by News Syndicate Co., Inc. Reg. U. S. Pat. Off.

Entered as 2nd class matter Post Office New York, N. Y.

Vol. 9. No. 133. 32 Pages New York, Monday, November 28, 1927 2 Cents

GRID GIANTS CAGE BEARS

Story on Page 28

(By Pacific & Atlantic)

THAT NOTRE DAME WIN!—Here's one of the thrilling scenes in that Chicago grid battle which Notre Dame won from University of Southern California by a 7—6 score—Capt. Drury of Trojans about to plunge through line. He was stopped by Walsh.

(NEWS photo)

GIANTS FRIGHTEN BEARS 13—7! — The New York Giants virtually clinched National league pro football honors by 13—7 beating they handed the Chicago Bears at Polo grounds yesterday. Jack McBride, who accounted for both Giant touchdowns, is shown (arrow) rushing through center for 3 yard gain in third period. *—Story on page 28.*

(NEWS photo)

The winner—Russell Jekel of the N. Y. A. C., who had handicap of 4 min. 30 sec., finished first.

Here are the leaders stepping along 1st ave. shortly after the start of the six-mile race (NEWS photo)

N. Y. A. C. LAD WINS EAST SIDE RACE!—With a handicap of 4 minutes and 30 seconds Russell Jekel, N. Y. A. C., won six-mile run of the First Avenue Boys yesterday. Tom Gregory took fast time prize and Mohawk A. C. won the team prize. *—Story on page 30.*

GIANTS UNSADDLE HORSEMEN

50,000 See Pros Outride Rockne's Squadron, 22-0, for Charity Fund

BY MARSHALL HUNT   DECEMBER 15, 1930

Notre Dame's famous Four Horsemen yesterday rode deep into the hearts of New Yorkers.

Their determined galloping on the flinty, bruising gridiron of the Polo Grounds was stopped abruptly by the professional Giants, 22 to 0, it is true, but, what is far more important, their valorous sorties and sallies against the siege of want and suffering were wholly successful.

More than 50,000 cheered every futile thrust of Knute Rockne's improvised squadron of former Notre Dame football players against the superb line of Tim Mara's team. It is probable that Mayor Walker's fund for the unemployed was swelled to the extent of $175,000, money that will be available immediately for the relief of 50,000 families in this city.

The skies were heavy with sullen clouds, and a biting wind was blowing from the north when the All-Stars kicked off to the Giants. A contest had begun in which Captain Benny Friedman of the Giants was to give one of his most effective and polished performances. He scored two of the three touchdowns made by the professionals and also fashioned an extra point with his talented kicking.

The Giants' third touchdown was scored in a spectacular way, Moran throwing a pass 30 yards to Comrade Campbell, who was standing in the end zone.

The Notre Dame All-Stars, with Commander Rockne sitting on the bench well blanketed, made only one first down and never once were in the Giants' territory.

But they went a long way into the feelings of this man's town.

FINAL EDITION

DAILY NEWS

NEW YORK'S PICTURE NEWSPAPER

Copyright, 1930, by News Syndicate Co., Inc. Reg. U. S. Pat. Off.

Entered as 2nd class matter Post Office, New York, N. Y.

THE LARGEST CIRCULATION IN AMERICA

Vol. 12. No. 147   52 Pages ★★★   New York, Monday, December 15, 1930   2 Cents IN CITY LIMITS | 3 CENTS Elsewhere

GIANTS 22, ALL STARS 0

—Story on Page 46

Up and at 'em! Pete Voedisch, Notre Dame '27, may not be as spry as he was back in the days when he was one of the Ramblers' star ends, but see him hurdle that line to stop Sedbrook, who has the ball. (NEWS photo)

They packed 'em in—50,000 of 'em. And that's $175,000 for charity!

HORSEMEN OUTRIDDEN. — Notre Dame's heroes, past and present, were blotted out, 22 to 0, by New York Giants at Polo grounds yesterday, but loudly huzzahed by throngs. —Story, p. 46.

He got even! Jack Elder intercepted Red Cagle's pass to beat the Army last year. And here's Red running with pass he stole from Jack in last quarter of yesterday's game. (NEWS photo)

The last Giant score—and a sensational one. Standing in the end zone, Campbell took a thirty-yard pass from Moran and then did this funny little flip as the rest of the boys rushed up. (NEWS photo)

BEARS RALLY TO DEFEAT GIANTS FOR TITLE, 23-21

DECEMBER 18, 1933

The New York Giants and Chicago's Bears met in Chicago today at Wrigley Field for the championship of the National Professional Football League. The Giants, champions of the Eastern Division, took a 7-6 lead over the Bears, Western title holders, at halftime. But the Bears scored a touchdown in the last few minutes of play and won, 23-21, as 25,000 witnessed the game.

The Bears took a 3 to 0 lead at the end of the first quarter on a field goal by Jack Manders.

Shortly after the second period started, the Giants got possession of the ball deep in their own territory. They smashed their way through the Bears' line and in four plays scored a touchdown.

The Giants' touchdown drive followed another field goal by Manders. The kick was made from the Giants' 40-yard line and it was the longest successful field goal in the league this season. The half ended with the Bears on their own nine-yard line with the score 7-6 in favor of the Giants.

The Bears regained the lead and were in front, 16-14, at the end of the third period.

Passes enabled the Giants to score again in the fourth quarter. Ken Strong kicked the extra point to give the Giants the lead, 21 to 16.

With the ball on the Giants' 35-yard line and five minutes to play, the Bears resorted to passing.

A triple pass, Molesworth to Hewitt to Karr, brought the Bears a touchdown in the final minutes. Ronsani then kicked the extra point and the Bears took the lead for good, 23 to 21. The final score: Bears 23, Giants 21.

TIM MARA (RIGHT), OWNER OF THE GIANTS, AND PITTSBURGH OWNER ART ROONEY COMPARE NOTES BEFORE THE 1933 NFL TITLE GAME. (DAILY NEWS)

GIANTS WIN TITLE, 30 TO 13

35,059 Thrilled Fans Mob Heroes and Cops

BY JACK MILEY   DECEMBER 10, 1934

A thrill-crazed crowd of 35,059 fans burst through Polo Grounds police barriers, engulfed the frozen field, and carried off splintered goalposts and bruised heroes of the New York Giants football team late yesterday afternoon. The Giants themselves provoked this riotous demonstration when they came from behind in a surging, heart-thumping drive to score four touchdowns in the last period and beat the hitherto undefeated Chicago Bears, 30 to 13, thereby winning the world's professional football championship.

Ken Strong, Ed Danowski, and Ike Frankian were the New York players strikingly responsible for this smashing upset, but these scoring athletes got plenty of cooperation from their teammates, and the Giants played like inspired men to turn what seemed like certain defeat into a glorious victory.

Strong made two touchdowns and Danowski and Frankian got one each. Danowski's rifling passes were brilliantly executed. The Fordham grad lugged that leather to town in the tough spots, and Strong was a human battering ram who outshone Chicago's Bronko Nagurski when he ripped and tore repeatedly through the Bears' beefy line.

Coach Steve Owen pulled a bit of strategy between halves that played an important part in the Giants' amazing comeback. Realizing that his chargers couldn't get a foothold for their cleated brogans on the rocklike playing field, he sent them back to battle wearing rubber-soled basketball shoes. The effect of this new footwear was magical. The Giant line held strong, while the charging Bears skidded futilely on the frozen terrain.

After trading in their slippery cleats for basketball sneakers in the second half, the Giants began overpowering the Bears in what has since become known as the famous "Sneakers Game." (Daily News)

LIONS LASH GIANTS FOR PRO TITLE, 26-7

DECEMBER 16, 1935

The Detroit Lions swept over a slippery gridiron here today to vanquish the New York Giants, 26 to 7, and thereby acquire their first National Professional Football Championship. A crowd of 13,000 persons sat through a light snowstorm to watch Detroit's professional gridders take up where the Detroit Tigers left off, to bring the Thorpe Memorial Trophy to the motor city for the first time.

Putting across a touchdown on the seventh play after the opening kickoff, the Lions remained ahead all the way. They outplayed the Giants in every department but kicking and passing, and in the latter the Lions were only outgained by a few yards.

Detroit scored a second touchdown later in the first period and two more in the closing minutes of the game.

New York tallied their only touchdown after five minutes of the third period. Danowski returned a Lion punt to the Detroit 46, and then slashed four yards off tackle. The ex-Fordham ace hurled a short pass that tipped Gutowski's fingers and settled into the waiting arms of Ken Strong. The Giant fullback galloped 30 yard across the goal line. Strong also converted from placement.

OPPOSITE: THE GIANTS' 1935 TITLE BOUT AGAINST THE LIONS WAS JUST ONE IN A LONG SERIES OF CHAMPIONSHIP GAMES FOR MEL HEIN (LEFT) AND COACH STEVE OWEN. HEIN AND PHIL SIMMS TOP THE GIANTS' LIST FOR MOST SEASONS AS AN ACTIVE PLAYER AT 15. OWEN SERVED AS THE GIANTS' HEAD COACH FOR 23 YEARS (1931-53), BY FAR THE LONGEST COACHING TENURE FOR THE GIANTS. (TOM WATSON, DAILY NEWS)

GIANTS RIP PACKERS, 23-17, FOR CROWN

BY JACK MAHON   DECEMBER 12, 1938

The Giants climaxed a brilliant season in spectacular fashion when they out-gamed a gallant, fighting band of Green Bay Packers, 23-17, to win the world's professional football championship for the second time, before 48,120 raving fans at the Polo Grounds yesterday. In a storybook game that had the crowd roaring from start to finish, the Giants struck fast, built up an early lead, lost it, and surged back through the gathering shadows for a sensational touchdown—and victory!

No movie director could have staged a better thriller. The teams, champs of the East and West, played their hearts out. The result was in doubt till the closing seconds, when Arnie Herber, alone under the floodlights, pitched a desperate, unsuccessful pass at Paul Miller.

Trailing, 17-16, after tossing away a 9-0 lead, the Giants came back in the third period to drive over the winning touchdown. After Engebretsen's 15-yard field goal had lifted the fighting Packers into their one-point lead, he kicked off to Howell, who returned to the Giants' 39.

Here the 61-yard march to victory began. Soar made 13 yards to the Packers' 39 and then bucked through his left side for eight more. Soar struggled to a first down on the 28. On the third down, Danowski faded, waited till Soar had cut over to the left, and rifled a bullet pass into his arms on the Packers' 7. Hinkle dove at Hank, grabbed his right leg, but couldn't pull him down.

Soar went over for a touchdown as the Polo Grounds went into one long roar. Cuff's placement made it 23-17, where, despite many Packer threats, it remained.

As rival Giants and Packers tangle, Clark Hinkle, Packers fullback (far left), attempts to gain yardage in the 1938 title game. (Daily News)

GIANTS CONQUER STARS, 13-10, ON CUFF'S FIELD GOAL

BY THE ASSOCIATED PRESS   **JANUARY 16, 1939**

Staging a brilliant finish to a hard-fought game, the Champion New York Giants knocked over the All-American All-Stars, 13-10, in a grand post-season finale to the pro grid season here today before 15,000.

Big Ed Danowski had just seen his great passing rival, Sammy Baugh, put the All-Stars in the lead with a spectacular pass, good for 70 yards. Then Danowski passed the Giants to a touchdown that tied it, 10-10.

As the final period wore on, the Giants stopped an All-Star drive led by Johnny Drake deep in their own territory and a moment later were inside the All-Star 20 after Ed Goddard had fumbled one of Danowski's punts.

With the ball on the 17, Ward Cuff, burly Giant back, won the game with a field goal.

The first period produced no scores. In the next, Johnny Karcis set the stage for a Giant score by intercepting a pass in midfield and running it to the All-Star 13. On the fourth down, Feets Barnum rushed into the game and booted the ball through the uprights.

Ed Goddard, former Washington State star, engineered the All-Stars from his own 35 to a spot downfield where big Ernie Smith, his tackle, tied the score with a field goal from the 26-yard line with less than 20 seconds of the half to go.

In the third, ex-Nebraska back Cardwell raced for a touchdown and Stydahar kicked the extra point to put the All-Stars ahead, 10-3.

The Giants were well on their way into All-Star territory as the last period began. Danowski's passes checked off 4, 8, 10, and 15 yards at a clip. The last one, good for 22, went to Gelatka, left end, and Cuff booted the tying point.

The win came after an All-Star fumble and Cuff's winning place kick.

AFTER CAPTURING THE 1938 NFL CHAMPIONSHIP, THE GIANTS PROVED THEIR SUPREMACY AGAIN WITH A WIN OVER THE ALL-AMERICAN ALL-STAR TEAM IN THE NFL'S FIRST-EVER PRO BOWL. HERE (FROM LEFT), GIANTS CAPTAIN MEL HEIN, OWNER TIM MARA, AND COACH STEVE OWEN CELEBRATE THE SEASON AT THE WHITEHALL HOTEL. (WALLY SEYMOUR, DAILY NEWS)

PACKERS TROUNCE GIANTS, 27-0, CAPTURE PRO GRID CHAMPIONSHIP

BY GENE WARD   DECEMBER 11, 1939

Green Bay's mighty Packers ground New York's Giants into the turf of State Fair Park here this blustery afternoon to become champions of the National Football League for the fifth time. The Giants never had a chance—everything they tried was wrong. Everything the Packers did was right. They ran and passed for three touchdowns, boomed over two field goals, and wound up with a 27-0 triumph—the most decisive margin ever registered in playoff competition. A milling, restless crowd of 32,279, which paid a record $83,510.35 at the gate, broke police lines in the final minutes and rimmed the gridiron on every side to heckle the Giants as they made a last desperate attempt to avert a shutout.

As they steamrollered their way to victory, the Packers stole all the Giants' thunder, making good use of the pass interception, a play for which the Giants have become famous. In all, the Green Bay boys stole six Giants aerials, two of these interceptions setting up touchdowns. The other Packer touchdown, scored by Milt Gantenbein on Arnie Herber's 7-yard pass, came after a 46-yard march in the first period.

The third-period touchdown was racked up on a Cecil Isbell to Joe Laws serial maneuver that covered 31 yards, and the fourth-period 6-pointer came when Ed Jankowski knifed the Giants' line from one yard out. Paul Engebretsen and Ernie Smith kicked the field goals and took care of the extra points.

OPPOSITE: DESPITE THEIR TROUNCING IN THE 1939 CHAMPION-SHIP GAME, THE GIANTS' SEASON HAD MANY GREAT VICTORIES TO CELEBRATE. HERE, ED DANOWSKI (LEFT) AND TUFFY LEEMANS TOAST THEIR 9-1-1 REGULAR-SEASON RECORD. (WALLY SEYMOUR, DAILY NEWS)

BEARS DEFEAT GIANTS, 37-9

Win Pro Title before Only 13,500

BY GENE WARD   DECEMBER 22, 1941

The Chicago Bears place-kicked their way from behind in the first half and ran the New York Giants right out of Wrigley Field in the second half today to clinch the professional football championship of the world by a score of 37-9. Only the accurate toe of Bob Snyder could combat the savage stubbornness of the Easterners in the opening half, but once the famed T-formation began to rumble, four straight touchdowns were chalked up by the Bear steamroller—two by Norm Standlee and one each by George McAfee and Ken Kavanaugh.

The Giants had the battle tied, 9-9, early in the third period, but that was the end of their gallant stand. Then, the quick bullet passes of Sid Luckman paved the way to the Bears' first touchdown; sheer, unadulterated power led to the second, and the breaks of the game set up the third and fourth.

The only surprise as the Bears became the first champions ever to repeat in the league's history was the slender turnout, only 13,500 fans showing up despite the fact that this probably is the Chicago team's last game as a unit. It was a terrific kick in the region of the players' pocketbooks, for the championship game is their game—the one in which they get a cut of the gate.

OPPOSITE: THE GIANTS' PLACE IN THE 1941 CHAMPIONSHIP GAME WAS NOT THE ONLY REASON FOR NEW YORKERS TO "JUMP FOR JOY" IN 1941. THE YANKEES' JOE DiMAGGIO CAPTIVATED FANS WITH HIS MAGICAL 56-GAME HITTING STREAK, AND THE 1941 WORLD SERIES FEATURED A YANKEES VICTORY OVER THE CROSSTOWN RIVAL BROOKLYN DODGERS. (TOM WATSON, DAILY NEWS)

GIANT BACKFIELDERS (LEFT TO RIGHT) HOWIE YEAGER, LELAND SCHAFFER, ANDY MAREFOS, AND MARION PUGH JUMP OVER THE NEW YORK LINE.

PACKERS CHAMPS!
DEFEAT GIANTS, 14-7

BY JACK SMITH   DECEMBER 18, 1944

The same rugged Green Bay Packers who bowed humbly to the Giants, 24-0, four weeks ago came slamming back into the Polo Grounds yesterday and cruised along a power-paved path to a 14-7 triumph over the same Giants and thus won the NFL championship. Before a shivering crowd of 46,016, the big bruisers from the little Wisconsin city battered through for two touchdowns in the second period, while the Giants, a feeble force throughout the first half, mustered their only scoring drive for a touchdown on the first play of the final quarter.

The crowd, which contributed gross gate receipts of $146,205.15 for a new league record, was disappointed in its hopes not only for a Giant victory but also for an abundance of thrills. It was not a spectacular game. Don Hutson, pass-catching ace of the Packers and the league's leading scorer for the fifth straight year, was a minor figure in the triumph. The Giants, crippled by the ineffectiveness of injured Blonde Bill Paschal, could not make their offense click at its sharpest.

Despite the valiant efforts of Ward Cuff, the Giant ground game was a no go. Howie Livingston vainly attempted to fill Paschal's shoes, but they were too big. This put the chief offensive burden on the venerable shoulders of Arnie Herber, and, despite the fact that his passes set up the lone Giant score, he was considerably off his normal, sharp stride.

As usual, the game was decided "up front," where this time the edge went to the Packers. They hit harder, faster, and more cleanly.

On defense, there was little to choose but that little went to the Packers. Sporadically, they succeeded in blotting out sections of the Giant wall and making way for their churning-legged backs to drive.

KEN STRONG, WITH THE BALL IN HIS HANDS, PLUNGES OVER THE GOAL
LINE FOR THE GIANTS' ONLY TOUCHDOWN IN THE 1944 TITLE GAME.
(PHOTO BY CHARLES HOFF, DAILY NEWS)

MEDAL FOR A GIANT HERO

1946

While our football heroes battle it out every Sunday for NFL glory, real heroes fight a much more important battle every day for the glory of our democracy. On that much bigger battlefield, a Giant rookie gave his life and earned the glory of our entire country.

First Lt. Jack Lummus was a rookie end for the Giants in 1941 before he enlisted in the Marines shortly after the foreign attack on Pearl Harbor. When U.S. troops shipped out for the Iwo Jima invasion in February 1945, Lummus was the commander of a platoon unit in the 5th Marine Division. After a few days of fighting, and enormous casualties on both sides, U.S. troops bravely raised the American flag on the Iwo Jima island.

Horrific fighting continued on the small island, where it was said that an advancement of 50 yards was a successful attack, and a gain of 100 yards a miracle. Proving the possibility of miracles, Lummus' platoon overcame three Japanese fortifications in the 48-hour period of March 6 and 7, 1945.

But on March 8th, while engaged in hand-to-hand combat with the enemy, Lummus was blown off his feet by a Japanese grenade. Not to be stopped, Lummus rose and continued his charge. This time, his shoulder was shattered by another Japanese grenade. Still commanding his men, Lummus charged forward and single-handedly destroyed two more enemy pillboxes.

After only a brief rest, Lummus led his men on their final charge, in what turned out to be his final act of heroism. As the platoon advanced, Lummus stepped on a land mine. Both his legs were ripped off, and his men looked on in shock as Lummus stood on his bloody stumps, still shouting commands to them. As their horror turned to rage, the platoon swept forward an unheard of 300 yards—a final tribute to their courageous leader.

Lummus lived a few hours more, and just before he died, he reportedly told a field surgeon, "I guess the New York Giants have lost the services of a damned good end."

On May 30, 1946, in the little town of Ennis, Texas, representatives of the military presented Lummus' mother with the Congressional Medal of Honor that President Harry S. Truman had conferred on First Lt. Jack Lummus.

In addition to Congressional Medal of Honor winner Jack Lummus (above), the Giants suffered the loss of former player Al Blozis, who was killed by German gunfire in France on January 31, 1945.

BEARS WALLOP GIANTS FOR CROWN, 24-14

BY GENE WARD   DECEMBER 16, 1946

Shocked by a gambling scandal which barred their only remaining fullback and racked by injuries throughout the opening half, the underdog Giants still battled the bruising Chicago Bears on even terms into the thrill-packed final period yesterday. At this point of a bitter fist-filled contest, and as 58,346 rooted for an upset from their chilly Polo Grounds pews, the weight and power of the invaders broke the 14-14 deadlock, and the Bears went on to win this record-smashing NFL championship by a 24-14 count.

One of the worst betting scandals since the notorious Black Sox fix of 1919 exploded yesterday when a Broadway salesman was arrested as the front man of a syndicate that tried to bribe two New York Giants players to throw the National Professional Football League title game.

The players police said were approached are:

Merle Hapes, hard-running fullback and the man the Giants had counted on yesterday because of injuries to other backfield stars. He was declared ineligible for the championship game and ducked out of sight. No charges were preferred against him.

Frank Filchock, ace passer, who came to the Giants from the Redskins at the start of the season. He was allowed to play.

Hapes was barred from playing because he had been approached directly, Football Commissioner Bert Bell said. The offer to Filchock was made by "innuendo," Bell added, and therefore he was allowed to take the field.

Jailed in lieu of $25,000 bail on charges of trying to bribe the players was Alvin J. Paris, 23. He called himself a salesman, but police said he was a bookmaker and front man for a "vicious" New Jersey gambling syndicate that had dabbled in trying to "fix" college sports.

FRANK FILCHOCK, WHO WAS CLEARED OF GAMBLING CHARGES THE DAY BEFORE THE 1946 CHAMPIONSHIP GAME, WATCHES THE ACTION FROM THE SIDELINES WITH COACH STEVE OWEN DURING THE GIANTS' 24-14 LOSS TO THE CHICAGO BEARS. (CHARLES HOFF, DAILY NEWS)

FOOTBALL GIANTS GET RIGHTS TO CONERLY

JANUARY 21, 1948

Draft rights to Charlie Conerly, the University of Mississippi's all-around star, were obtained yesterday by the New York Giants of the National Football League. In the process of rebuilding the club, which last season finished in the cellar, the Giants traded halfback Howie Livingston, four-season veteran, and an unnamed player to the Washington Redskins, who had the original draft rights to Conerly.

Conerly, who sparked Mississippi to the Southeastern Conference gridiron championship, established a collegiate aerial record last campaign by completing 133 of 233 passes. Also, his 57.1 percent average for completions was a new standard.

CONERLY'S RECORD WITH THE GIANTS
(1948-1961)

#2 MOST PASSES ATTEMPTED, CAREER—2,833

#2 MOST PASSES ATTEMPTED, GAME—53 ON DECEMBER 5, 1948

#2 MOST PASSES COMPLETED, CAREER—1,418

#2 MOST PASSES COMPLETED, GAME—36 ON DECEMBER 5, 1948

#2 MOST YARDS PASSING, CAREER—19,488

#2 MOST TOUCHDOWN PASSES, CAREER—173

#2 MOST CONSECUTIVE GAMES, TOUCHDOWN PASSES—10

Charlie Conerly ranks among the best Giant quarterbacks of all time. (Daily News)

GIANTS DROP T, POUND CARDS BY RECORD 51-21

BY GENE WARD   NOVEMBER 13, 1950

The faces of Curly Lambeau and his Cardinals were redder than their scarlet shirts in the Polo Grounds yesterday. Deceitful Steve Owen had his Giants pull a low-down, sneaky switch from the T-formation to his old A-style single wing, and the result was a horrendous hiding of the Chicago crew by a 51-21 count, the Giant total being the biggest score they've run up since 1933.

If there were any certified public accountants in the crowd of 22,380, they knew the Giants had scored seven touchdowns, kicked six conversions and a 20-yard field goal. A rush to the record books by Giant figure filberts dug up information that the Polo Grounds gang hadn't gone over the 50 mark offensively since they clipped the Eagles, 56-0, 17 years ago.

With more blocking power ahead of the runner and more protection for the passer, the Giants really ripped. Choo Choo Roberts, moving into the fullback slot, chugged for 218 yards on 26 carries and produced two touchdowns on romps of 63 and 35 yards. His ground-gaining hit a new Giant high, erasing Bill Paschal's old mark of 188.

That Mississippi man, Chuck Conerly, an old single-wing operator who never has been at home in the T, gloried in his old formation by completing 10 out of 20 aerials for 234 yards and two TDs.

As for his catchers, they were Columbia Bill Swiacki with six completions for 12 yards and a touchdown; Bob McChesney with two for 58 yards and a touchdown.

OPPOSITE: JOE SCOTT, GIANT HALFBACK, SLAMS OVER THE GOAL LINE EARLY IN THE SECOND PERIOD FOR ONE OF THE GIANTS' SEVEN TOUCHDOWNS AGAINST THE CARDINALS. CHOO CHOO ROBERTS SCORED TWO OF THE TEAM'S TOUCHDOWNS AND GAINED 218 YARDS—STILL THE GIANTS' RECORD FOR YARDS GAINED IN A SINGLE GAME. (CHARLES HOFF, DAILY NEWS)

ROTE TO GIANTS IN GRID DRAFT

JANUARY 19, 1951

The Giants and Steve Owen plucked the prize plum of the National Football League's annual college draft today in Southern Methodist's Kyle Rote, but the Bears and Eagles came up with more first-choice manpower for a wartime future.

Stout Steve Owen, veteran Giant coach, was the sixth club representative to draw for the "bonus" choice. He won first pick and chose Rote, four-year veteran of the Mustangs.

"He was great in the East-West game," Owen said, "and then he played a great game against us in the Senior Bowl."

Rote was eyed by six of the nine teams eligible for the bonus selection. He played fullback in the T-formation in the East-West game and was single-wing tailback for SMU, thus fitting in with the Giants' T-and-A formation attack.

ROTE'S RESUME WITH THE GIANTS (1951-1961)

#1   MOST RECEIVING TOUCHDOWNS, CAREER—48
#1   MOST CONSECUTIVE GAMES, TOUCHDOWN RECEPTIONS—7
#8   MOST CONSECUTIVE GAMES, PASS RECEPTIONS—23
#5   MOST RECEPTIONS, CAREER—300
#10 MOST TOTAL POINTS, CAREER—312

FOUR-TIME PRO BOWL SELECTION—1954-57

During Kyle Rote's 11-year career with the Giants, he helped lead the franchise to four NFL Championship games, including the title in 1956. (Daily News)

PRICE IS HIGH AS GIANTS BLAST PAST EAGLES, 23-7

BY GENE WARD   DECEMBER 10, 1951

Exploding on an 80-yard scoring blast and accumulating 171 yards through and around the weary, old Eagles, young sophomore fullback Eddie Price rollicked to a new Giant single-season ground-gaining record here yesterday, as he paced his mates to a 23-7 triumph.

There was only one sour note—Steve Owen's offense didn't catch fire until too late in the season, and in Pittsburgh, the Cleveland Browns were sewing up the American Conference crown.

Price cut loose his long-range wallop on the first play from scrimmage following the Eagles' lone touchdown in the second period. It was a pitchout from Chuck Conerly, and Eddie, tucking the leather in the crook of his arm, cut back over the Eagle right tackle, broke loose from two tacklers, then outraced Jay MacDowell to pay dirt.

At 12:59 of the second period, the Giants went in front for keeps as Ray Poole arched a 41-yard field goal between the uprights. It was the veteran end's first of three for the day—a trio which give him 10 three-pointers for the campaign and another new Giant mark. The old field-goal season record was eight, set by Ben Agajanian in 1949.

As for Price, the 171 yards that this ex-Tulane 26-year-old piled up during his greatest day in pro ball brought his 1951 total to 833 yards, erasing by three yards the standard set by Tuffy Leemans in 1936. And Eddie still has another game to go.

OPPOSITE: THE NEW YORK GIANTS' OFFENSE WAS POWERED BY FULLBACK EDDIE PRICE (31), WHO GAINED A THEN-SINGLE-SEASON RECORD OF 971 YARDS IN 1951. (WALLY SEYMOUR, DAILY NEWS)

WHAT'S WRONG WITH N.Y. SPORTS?

BY GENE WARD   JANUARY 19, 1954

The New York football Giants haven't won a divisional crown since 1946 or an NFL title since 1938. Their attendance suffered a 25% sag last fall when they won but three of 12 games . . . their coach has been relieved of his command after 23 years . . . and the bulwark of their defensive unit, all-league tackle Arnie Weinmeister, has quit the club to complete his career in Canada.

What's wrong with this once all-powerful gridiron organization? This question has been the subject of heated debate since early last Fall.

New York football fans only know what they see each Sunday at the Polo Grounds or on their TV screens when the Giants are on the road. And, as the saying goes, "It ain't been good."

The clan Mara—Jack, the president and treasurer; Wellington, the secretary and talent scout; and Tim, not quite the silent partner he now pretends to be—evidently felt the main fault lay with the coaching.

So, Steve Owen was asked to resign, move upstairs to make way—everybody thought—for a young, progressive head coach or, at the very least, a big-name gate attraction. After all, this was New York . . . the Big Apple.

Jim Lee Howell, who had been only a part-time assistant to Owen—not even his No.1 lieutenant—scarcely fills the bill on either count. Since his appointment, there has been an apparent division of command, with Army's backfield coach, Vince Lombardi, moving in ostensibly to help Howell mold a new offense.

What they can accomplish—presuming adequate material, of course—depends on staff harmony. Kyle Rote is going to make quite a bit more money the next three years than either Howell or Lombardi, and the latter may be making the same amount as head coach Howell himself. For that matter, Chuck Conerly made more than Owen, but no one can say that the Mississippi man didn't labor for his pay.

The future remains to be told, and the debate lingers on.

Bringing in the great Vince Lombardi in 1954 to help revamp the Giants' offense helped stem the tide of losing and spurred the team to a championship run in the 1950s and early 1960s that few teams have ever duplicated. (Daily News)

THE POWERHOUSE

The Giants' Alex Webster

BY JIMMY POWERS   NOVEMBER 7, 1955

Said Lou Little: "The Giants' Alex Webster is the finest broken-field runner I've seen since—well, since Cliff Battles. He has a remarkable ability to cut, veer, and change directions without losing speed."

Said Jim Lee Howell: "Webster is unquestionably the best running halfback in this business. I've said this all along—Webster runs very much like Tuffy Leemans. But he's much faster than Tuffy."

Both coaches were speaking at the Football Writers luncheon. Against the Washington Redskins, Webster gained 136 yards running and pass catching, scored two touchdowns, and had been voted the game's best offensive player.

The object of these accolades is a tall, friendly young man with close cropped reddish hair. Watching him walk across the room to shake hands, an interviewer is likely to feel that there is little in his ambling gait and almost sheepish grin to suggest the power he displays when hitting into the line on Sunday afternoons.

Webster signed to play with the Giants last winter following two seasons with the Montreal Alouettes of the Canadian League. In '54 he led his league in touchdowns, ball carrying, and scoring; was named most valuable back in the circuit; and was voted "Most Popular" of the Alouettes by the fans.

Now he leads the Giants in ball carrying with 65 attempts for 360 yards and a 5.5-yards - per-try average. He leads the team also in pass catching with 17 receptions, good for 220 yards. He is third in scoring. He won the "Best on Offense" prize in two of the three games for which it was awarded.

"Webster is a lot like Ward Cuff," recalls Little. Cuff, a halfback, played nine years with the Giants. "One week Cuff had a throat infection and reported before the game with a 103 fever. He hadn't been able to eat all week, and now he tells me he intends to play. I told him I would not permit it, but to keep him quiet, I finally allowed him to be treated by the trainers and to dress."

ALEX WEBSTER GETS A PLAYER'S VIEW OF THE GIANTS' BATTLE-FIELD—THE POLO GROUNDS. (WALKER KELLEHER, DAILY NEWS)

56,836 SEE GIANTS RIP BEARS, 47-7

BY GENE WARD   DECEMBER 31, 1956

The Bears once clobbered a title tilt foe, 73-0, and it has stood through the years as the perfection in offensive football. Now the once-mighty Monsters of the Midway know how it feels to be on the receiving end, for yesterday they were ground into the icy terrain of Yankee Stadium, their spirits spattered and their bodies battered, as the tremendous team play of the Giants produced an all but unbelievable 47-7 triumph and brought New York its first professional football championship in 18 years.

This is a story which could have been written long before halftime. The Giants had come into the arena as one of the most fired-up clubs ever to trod a gridiron anywhere. Inspiration was the word for it as they shattered the Chicago defenses for 13 points in the first period and 21 in the second.

The impossible was taking place out there on the field, and the fans forgot the numbing 22-degree chill and the biting wind that whipped through the girdered tiers of the stadium. They put their lungs into a demonstration which mounted in intensity through the bitter day as the Giants piled humiliation after humiliation on the Bears.

Playing as though they had wings on their sneakers, the Giants slammed to a 34-7 halftime bulge. And the pessimists who were worrying about a second-half letdown needn't have, for the Bears had had it, but good.

There was an incident in the third period which told the whole story of this Giants team. Frank Gifford, just one of a multitude of heroes, had pulled off a brilliant run. The score at the moment was 40-7, but as he picked himself up, his mates rushed over to congratulate him.

In the face of such unity, the Bears were helpless, and the Giants, atoning for three previous championship beatings by the Bears, achieved success beyond the rosiest dreams of their most avid rooters.

FANS AT YANKEE STADIUM ENDURED NUMBING COLD CONDITIONS AS THEY WATCHED THEIR GIANTS DEFEAT THE CHICAGO BEARS FOR THE TEAM'S FIRST CHAMPIONSHIP IN 18 YEARS. (FRANK HURLEY, DAILY NEWS)

HIS COACHES SAY ROSEY BROWN IS MAYBE THE GREATEST EVER

BY HARRY CRONIN   NOVEMBER 10, 1957

A questioner was pushing John Dell Isola to compare youthful All-Pro Roosevelt Brown with some of the great linemen he has seen. Dell Isola is a former All-Pro himself, and his big-time experience goes back a quarter-century. That era covers Hein, Fortmann, Stydahar, Turner . . . why go on?

"I don't want to say," said the Giants line coach, with a grin and a quick glance in Brown's direction. "I don't want him to get an inflated head." Then, having relented or let his thoughts mature on the subject, Dell Isola said:

"The only lineman that even came close to him as a downfield blocker was Ed Widseth.

"Remember," John muttered softly as he left the room. "I said: 'Even came close.'"

His coaches give him a wide margin over any offensive lineman now active in the league. The difference between Rosey and other top tackles, like Lou Creekmur of Detroit and Mike McCormick of the Browns, is Rosey's speed.

Rosey, in action, is a fine illustration of the fact that modern pro ball is a game of physical coordination, rather than brute strength. He seems well contained in his moves and even throws a rolling block with a light ease and grace.

"In my first year with the pros, I tried to rely on strength and took an awful beating. Now I resort to tricks," he says.

"On difficult assignments like pitchouts," offensive coach Vince Lombardi says, "Brown gets out there with the fast block you need. He's extremely quick in pulling out of the line. He's in a class by himself at getting downfield under kicks. He has the largest forearms in the league, loads of desire, and he's durable."

Rosey is as mild a man as he is large, and gets mad at somebody "on the average of once during a game."

"When that happens, I just block 'em a little harder," he says.

PICKED IN THE 27TH ROUND OF THE 1953 DRAFT BY THE GIANTS,
ROSEY BROWN WENT ON TO EARN PRO BOWL HONORS NINE TIMES
AND WAS ENSHRINED IN PRO FOOTBALL'S HALL OF FAME IN 1975.
(DAILY NEWS)

CAMERA SPY GIANTS' 12TH MAN

BY DICK YOUNG   DECEMBER 14, 1957

That guy in the upper deck of Yankee Stadium every football Sunday, taking pictures with a jazzed-up Polaroid camera, isn't Steve Allen—or even Jack Paar. And he's not doing a commercial.

It's Wellington Mara, snapping the enemy defenses and "smuggling" the results down onto the field so that the Giants can exploit the information obtained.

"It's a tremendous help to us," says offense coach Vince Lombardi. "I have great faith in its value."

The younger Mara, born and bred to football, heads a veritable spy ring. Operating with him are Ken Kavanaugh, a messenger, and Lombardi. Kavanaugh, the end coach, works alongside Mara, high in the Stadium. Ken operates the phone. When he spots a hot situation, he phones the bench and alerts them.

"They're using a different defense than we expected from the scouting reports," he'll say. "We're shooting down a picture on it."

Some 30 seconds later, the picture is in the hands of Lombardi on the Giant bench, where it is examined and analyzed.

"The quality of the photograph isn't so hot," Mara grins. "We don't take the normal 60 seconds to develop a print, because we're in a hurry. And we stuff the wet print into the sock and it gets scratched. But we're not after any Oscar for photographic excellence. We're just after information."

There's one drawback. "We couldn't use it in Philly when we played there at night," Mara says. "They haven't come up with a film that's sensitive enough to be used at night."

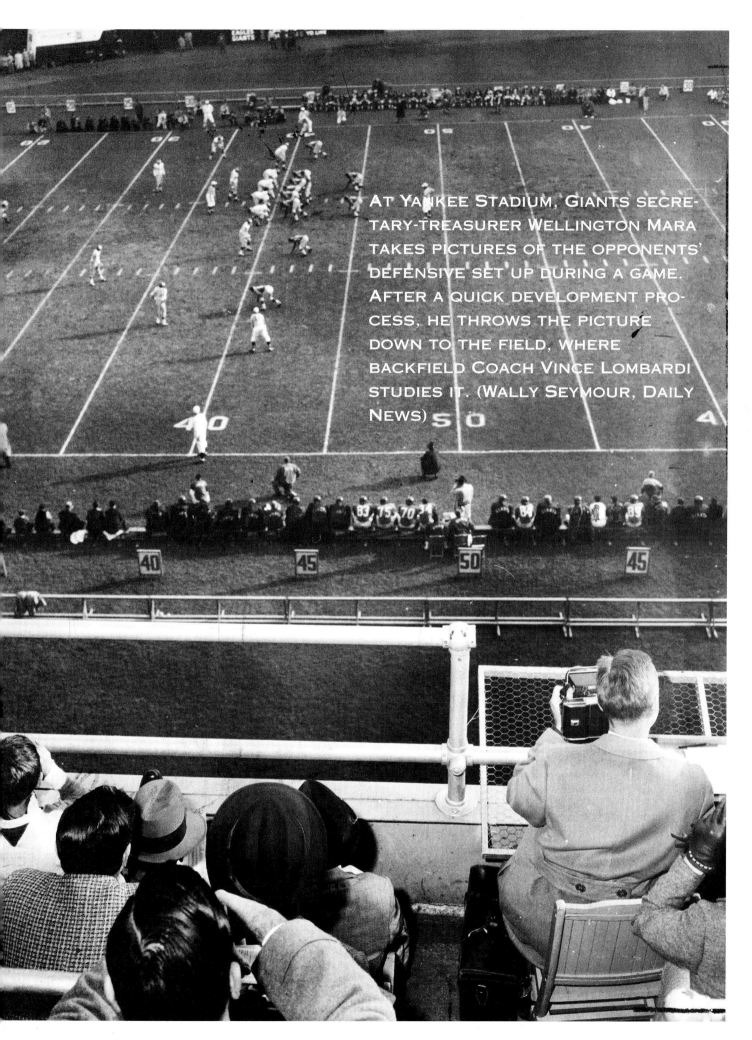

At Yankee Stadium, Giants secretary-treasurer Wellington Mara takes pictures of the opponents' defensive set up during a game. After a quick development process, he throws the picture down to the field, where backfield Coach Vince Lombardi studies it. (Wally Seymour, Daily News)

GIANTS (CONERLY) TRIP BROWNS, 21-17

Charlie Pitches 3 TD Passes

BY GENE WARD   NOVEMBER 3, 1958

There are 78,404 fans with black crepe-paper expressions filing out of this lakefront arena. They have just witnessed the impossible. Their mighty Browns, touted as the greatest machine ever assembled in the reign of moleskin magician Paul Brown, have just gone down in a 21-17 defeat before the Giants.

It couldn't happen . . . but it did! The Giants—racked by injuries and playing without their bread-and-butter halfback, Frank Gifford, their best offensive guard, Jack Stroud, and No. 1 quarterback Don Heinrich—had swarmed from behind for third- and fourth-period touchdowns to plaster the Browns with their first defeat of the campaign in an upset of upsets.

This crowd, the biggest a Giant team ever has played before, still can't believe the scoreboard.

And the guy who burst the bubble was none other than Charlie Conerly—ancient, discredited Chucking Chuck, the old man of the league who, just two short weeks ago, was booed to the bench by his own fans in Yankee Stadium.

The 37-year-old from Ole Miss, in his 11th campaign, went the distance on the mound. He fired 23 passes, completing 12 for 194 yards and all three Giant touchdowns. He pitched for the first tally at 7:15 of the second period to move the Giants in front, 7-3; the second at 4:45 of the third to pull the Giants to within three points at 17-14; and the third at 2:50 of the fourth for the winner.

He had plenty of help: Alex Webster carried the load at halfback, Bob Schnelker glued himself to Conerly's first TD throw, and fullback Mel Triplett outgained the mighty Jim Brown, 116 yards to 113. For these rabid Cleveland fans, this was the unkindest cut of all.

THE GIANTS' 1958 UPSET OF THE CLEVELAND BROWNS RANKS AS ONE OF
THE GREATEST UPSETS IN FRANCHISE HISTORY. SHOWN HERE ARE MEM-
BERS OF THAT GIANT SQUAD, (L TO R), ALEX WEBSTER, CHARLIE CONERLY,
MEL TRIPLETT, AND FRANK GIFFORD. (ED PETERS, DAILY NEWS)

GIANTS STOP COLTS, 24-21, TIE FOR 1ST

71,163 See Summerall's Winning FG

BY GENE WARD   NOVEMBER 10, 1958

Old Man Conerly and his young Giant teammates did it again yesterday! Before New York's biggest professional football crowd—a whooping, pleading, hoarse-voiced 71,163 stacked in Yankee Stadium—the Giants exploded their second successive upset of an unbeaten team. They bounced the Colts, 24-21, to tie their victims of the previous Sunday, the Browns, for the Eastern Division lead.

Down, 14-7, to a moleskin machine that had pulverized six straight rivals by runaway scores, the Giants slashed their way to a brace of third-period tallies. Then, in a heart-pounding final 15 minutes, they lost the lead, stopped another Baltimore assault, and drove to within field-goal range for the winning kick on Conerly's clutch aerials and the ramming runs of Frank Gifford and Phil King.

It was fourth down and 3 to go at the Baltimore 21 when lanky Pat Summerall took position for the payoff boot—and his 28-yard kick sailed high and true over the uprights with two minutes 40 seconds remaining on the clock.

This dramatic drive for field-goal position was packed with heroic play. It stemmed from a key interception of a George Shaw aerial by linebacker Sam Huff as the Colts made a tremendous bid to break the deadlock and preserve their all-winning record. They were unsuccessful, though, and the mighty Giants prevailed.

OPPOSITE: PAT SUMMERALL'S 28-YARD FIELD GOAL SEALED THE GIANTS' 24-21 WIN OVER THE COLTS AND MOVED THE NEW YORKERS INTO A TIE FOR FIRST PLACE IN THE EASTERN DIVISION. (DAILY NEWS)

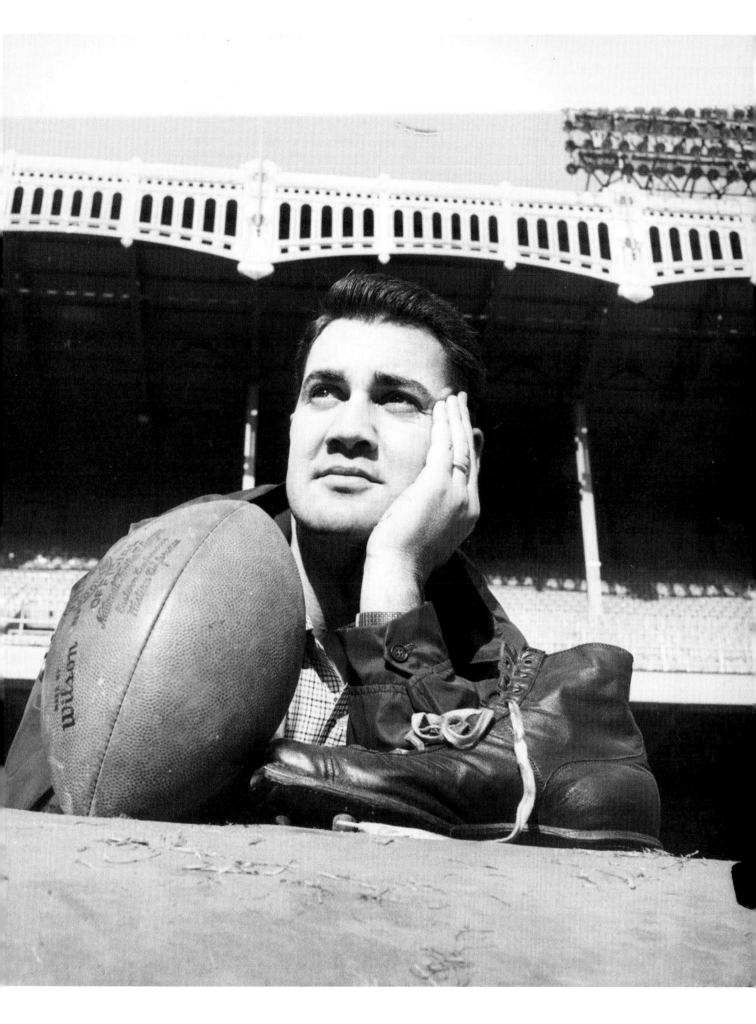

THE FOUR COMMANDOS

One of the All-Time Great Defensive Units, Giants Forwards Specialize in Demolition behind Enemy Lines

BY HARRY CRONIN   NOVEMBER 23, 1958

Football has had its Seven Mules, Seven Blocks, and Suicide Seven. The Colts currently boast a mighty veteran echelon referred to by scout Jack Lavelle as "the four fastest bellies in the National League," though in Baltimore they are more reverently known as the Ferocious Four. But the Giants forwards, while gaining recognition as one of the greatest lines of all time, are as yet still known as just four guys named Andy, Rosey, Mo, and Kat.

In carrying out their mission, Andy, Rosey, Mo, and Kat rely on cuteness and quickness, pin-pointing the play rather than bashing everything in sight, as other great lines have done. Maybe, since their specialty is demolition behind enemy lines, they should be called the Four Commandos.

At the Stadium, the fondest cheers ring out when the defense trots to the bench after smearing an enemy passer and forcing a punt. Sometimes the offense will reward their efforts with a fumble and the doughty rushers will have to return to the fray with their backs to the goal line. Even then, the customers take heart that trouble may be averted if the infiltrators can nail the passer for a long loss.

A bad day is just never on the calendar for the firm of Andy, Rosey, Mo, and Kat. On a given afternoon, the pass defense may look like a sieve, the protection a paper screen, the carriers may eat grass, and Charlie Conerly may not be able to toss a pinball through a hula hoop. But that Giant line never lets the customers down. Andy and Kat contain 'em, Rosey and Mo brain 'em.

The Four Commandos were forged together in 1956, when they provided the missing element in the Giants' quest for their first division title since 1946 and first world championship since '38.

THE GIANTS' FAMED FOUR COMMANDOS (LEFT TO RIGHT), ROSEY GRIER,
DICK MODZELEWSKI, JIM KATCAVAGE, AND ANDY ROBUSTELLI, TALK
AFTER PRACTICE IN FRONT OF YANKEE STADIUM. (DAVID MCLANE, DAILY
NEWS)

COLTS WIN IN SUDDEN DEATH, 23-17

Cop Title in Fifth Period after Late FG Ties Giants

BY GENE WARD   DECEMBER 29, 1958

In the years to come, when our children's children are listening to stories about football, they'll be told about the greatest game ever played—the one between the Giants and Colts for the 1958 NFL championship.

They'll be told of heroics the likes of which never had been seen...of New York's slashing two-touchdown rally to a 17-14 lead...of Baltimore's knot-tying field goal seven seconds from the end of regulation playing time...and, finally, of the bitter collapse of the magnificent Giant defense as the Colts slammed and slung their way to a 23-17 triumph with an 80-yard touchdown drive in the first sudden-death period ever played.

"Once upon a time, on an unbelievably balmy day in the middle of a long, fierce cold spell . . ." That's the way the story will begin, only the kids won't believe a word of it, because what transpired on the sacred sod of Yankee Stadium yesterday had the weird and wonderous quality of a Grimm fairy tale. Even the 64,185 fans who were there, nerves twisted and frayed by the swift-changing tides of battle, aren't quite certain it all happened the way that it did.

There were sensational aerial maneuvers and hard-nosed goal-line stands. There was the tremendous 86-yard forward-pass-and-fumble play by the Conerly-Rote-Webster combo, which led to the first Giant touchdown, and the terrific pitch-and-catch antics of the Johnny Unitas-Ray Berry duo for a new championship record.

There were all these heart-pounding plays, and more. But a little line buck on a third-down play in the dying minutes of the fourth period, which fell six inches short, proved the pivot on which victory swung in the richest NFL championship in history. This classic grossed $698,646, including receipts from television and radio, and resulted in fame for the winning and losing players.

ALAN AMECHE'S TOUCHDOWN PLUNGE IN OVERTIME ENDED THE "GREAT-EST GAME EVER PLAYED" AND LAUNCHED THE NFL ON ITS CLIMB TO OVERTAKE BASEBALL AS AMERICA'S NATIONAL PASTIME. (AP/WIDE WORLD PHOTOS)

THOUSANDS OF GRID FANS RIOT AT STADIUM

BY JOE TRIMBLE   DECEMBER 7, 1959

Thousands of fans stormed down from the Yankee Stadium stands just before the end of yesterday's game, and mob hysteria took over. A riot ensued and special details of police had to be called to put down the senseless demonstration. The Giants were leading, 48-7.

The Cleveland Browns refused to continue to play—a minute and about fifty seconds remained in the game—and left the field. When they moved out, the game was halted, and then the mobs really went wild. They stormed over the field, pushing and fighting. The Giant substitutes grouped together on the sidelines to defend themselves.

The trouble started when about 200 stormed the north goalpost toward left field. They were dispersed by special cops and ushers, and then other hundreds poured out of the first-base stands and uprooted the posts at that end of the field.

The game was first delayed for 20 minutes while the police cleared the field. Actually, they could only get the hooligans off the gridiron. Swirling mobs of drunks and delinquents then continued the fights in the outfield section in right field.

Referee Harry Brubaker said, "It was the worst I've ever seen. I had a similar experience a couple of years ago in San Francisco, but this was worse."

Jim Lee Howell, Giants coach, said:

"They were mixing in among our players, pushing and milling. There were a lot of drunks. They were well-wishers and it's nice to have fans, but they were too excited. I feared my own players might be hurt, too. And I was afraid of a forfeit. After having won it, I didn't want to lose that way."

The game ended with the gridiron completely ringed by spectators and with only the left-field goalpost still upright. This was leveled a few seconds after the final gun.

ALTHOUGH THE RIOT AT YANKEE STADIUM ENDED THE GAME PREMATURELY,
THE GIANTS' 48-7 LEAD OVER THE CLEVELAND BROWNS STOOD AS THE FI-
NAL SCORE AND PUSHED THE NEW YORKERS TO THE TOP SPOT IN THE
NFL's EASTERN DIVISION. (DAILY NEWS)

COLTS CLOBBER GIANTS FOR TITLE, 31-16

Unitas Triggers 24-Point Explosion in Last Period

BY GENE WARD   DECEMBER 28, 1959

For a span of 10 minutes 21 seconds here in tension-packed Memorial Stadium—from midway of the third period to the third minute of the fourth—the outmanned, underdog Giants had the Colts whipped, three field goals to one touchdown. But they were living on borrowed time, hanging by their fingernails on the edge of a mighty cliff, with 57,545 screaming, pleading Baltimore rooters waiting for them to fall. When they fell, it was with a mighty crash which buried them under an avalanche of Colt touchdowns and a 31-16 defeat.

To win their second straight NFL crown, the Colts exploded for four touchdowns and a field goal in a fiery fourth-period uprising that turned this concrete saucer into a bedlam.

The back of this gutty but futile Giant stand was broken by an 85-yard, 10-play drive engineered by that hot-fingered aerial genius, Johnny Unitas, who capped this smashing offense by whirling the final four yards for the touchdown and a 14-9 Baltimore bulge.

What happened next will live in the nightmares of the Giants and their followers through the long, bitter winter. In the space of 10 minutes, the Colts completely wrecked the Giants with a 24-point deluge, and the turmoil of the conquering mob must have been discernible way back in New York.

OPPOSITE: CENTURY MILSTEAD (FAR LEFT), A MEMBER OF THE ORIGINAL 1925 GIANTS, LINES UP WITH THE TEAM'S 1959 OFFENSIVE BRAINTRUST (LEFT TO RIGHT): HEAD COACH JIM LEE HOWELL, QUARTERBACK CHARLIE CONERLY, AND ASSISTANT COACH ALLIE SHERMAN. DESPITE LOSING THE 1959 TITLE GAME, THE GIANTS CAPPED OFF THE 1950S WITH ANOTHER GREAT SEASON, FINISHING ATOP THE EASTERN CONFERENCE WITH A 10-2 REGULAR-SEASON RECORD. (CHARLES HOFF, DAILY NEWS)

EAGLE GAME INJURIES FINISH GIFF FOR YEAR

BY GENE WARD   NOVEMBER 22, 1960

Frank Gifford, bread-and-butter ball player for the Giants, is through for the season.

This was the sad state of affairs yesterday in the wake of the Eagles' 17-10 come-from-behind triumph in Yankee Stadium, and the Giants' 3 1/2-point favorites for last Sunday's battle now are 5 1/2-point underdogs for the one coming up.

Although there were charges from some quarters that Chuck Bednarik's block-busting shoulder tackle, which knocked Gifford loose from his senses and the football to break up a last-ditch drive for the equalizing touchdown, was a "foul blow," the great Giant halfback couldn't debate the issue himself.

Giff was lying in St. Elizabeth's Hospital, where he was taken directly from the Stadium, and he didn't have the wisp of a memory left about any portion of the game.

He didn't remember Bednarik's high, "blind-side" tackle at the Eagle 30 as he raced toward a corner. He didn't even recall dressing for battle.

There isn't the slightest chance Gifford can play again this year. The doctor was emphatic on that point. "He will be kept in the hospital for at least three weeks, and there will be no visitors and no photographers."

Giff himself still had a bad headache, but he was chipper enough to call for his shaving gear and to tell Maxine, his wife, that he wanted out of the hospital. He wasn't yet informed the doctor's orders were for a somewhat longer stay.

PHILADELPHIA'S CHUCK BEDNARIK'S VIOLENT HIT ON FRANK GIFFORD LEFT THE GIANT STAR UNCONSCIOUS AND IN THE HOSPITAL FOR OVER TWO WEEKS. THE FAMOUS HIT "KNOCKED" GIFFORD INTO A ONE-YEAR RETIREMENT. REFLECTING BACK, ALL PARTIES AGREE THAT THE HIT WAS "CLEAN," WITH THE GIANTS' SAM HUFF GOING SO FAR AS TO CALL IT "THE FINEST TACKLE I'VE EVER SEEN." (DAILY NEWS)

GRID GIANTS DEALT TITTLE

BY JIM McCULLEY   AUGUST 16, 1961

The New York football Giants engineered one of the big deals of the off-season yesterday when they acquired Y.A. Tittle, 34, veteran quarterback, from the San Francisco Forty-Niners.

In return, the Giants had to give up one of the NFL's most promising young offensive linemen, 23-year-old Lou Cordileone, who was their No. 1 draft pick in '60.

It was a straight swap, with no cash or future draft choices involved, according to Ray Walsh, GM of the New York club.

"We feel we are getting one of the great quarterbacks in the NFL," Walsh said. "It wasn't easy to part with Cordileone, but if you want something good, you have to give up something good. We were fortunate to be able to get a quarterback as good as Tittle. The idea of acquiring Tittle didn't seem possible at first, but there it is."

And with Tittle arriving on the scene, where does that leave 40-year-old Chuck Conerly? "Conerly is still our No. 1 quarterback," said Walsh. "But it would be utterly foolish to expect Chuck to play every minute of a rugged 14-game schedule. Tittle is insurance, the finest we could obtain, that Conerly won't have to be asked to play a 14-game schedule."

Tittle made a fine showing against the Giants in the Forty-Niners' 21-20 loss in an exhibition game at Portland last Saturday night. He probably will get his first action as a Giant when the club meets the Rams at Los Angeles Saturday.

OPPOSITE: OUTLINED AGAINST THE GLOOMY MIST OF YANKEE STADIUM, Y.A. TITTLE WALKS TO THE SIDELINES. EVEN THOUGH TITTLE WAS ACQUIRED BY THE GIANTS LATE IN HIS HALL OF FAME CAREER, HE HOLDS MANY OF THE TEAM'S OFFENSIVE RECORDS, INCLUDING HIGHEST CAREER PASSING EFFICIENCY (55.89), MOST TOUCHDOWN PASSES IN A SEASON (36 IN 1963) AND MOST TOUCHDOWN PASSES IN A GAME (7), WHICH IS STILL AN NFL RECORD. (DAILY NEWS)

PACKERS OVERWHELM GIANTS, 37-0

Record 19 for Hornung in Title Tilt

BY GENE WARD   JANUARY 1, 1962

Let's face it and start the New Year right with the truth—our Giants not only were beaten here today, but they were disgraced, as the Packers took the NFL championship in a 37-0 romp.

With Paul Hornung, their Fort Riley soldier boy, collecting 19 points for a playoff scoring record and quarterback Bart Starr stealing the Giants' aerial thunder with three touchdown tosses, the Packers exploded in a 21-point second period and wound up handing the spiritless New Yorkers their worst title-game thumping in 13 playoff appearances.

Not since 1953, when the Steelers slugged them, 63-7, in a regular-season game, have the Giants taken such a hosing; not since 1953, when the Browns hung a goose-egg on them, have they been shut out. The worst of it is, the Eastern Division champs didn't appear to have an excuse in the world for a showing which amazed even the most rabid of the 39,029 in City Stadium.

What had been billed as a mighty match between rushing power and aerial accuracy came apart at the seams in the second period as the Packers stormed to three touchdowns in the space of 10 minutes flat.

It was the 12th championship outing for the Giants and their ninth shellacking. Going into the battle, they were all even with the Packers at 1-and-1 in title tiffs, having whipped them, 23-17, in 1938 and been whipped, 14-7, in 1944. This time, they were up against a team that could do no wrong.

OPPOSITE: DURING THE EARLY 1960S, THE GIANTS' VAUNTED AIR ATTACK WAS PROTECTED BY 1,250 POUNDS OF OFFENSIVE LINEMAN. SHOWING THEIR STANDOUT FORM ARE (LEFT TO RIGHT), REED BOHOVICH, JACK STROUD, BOOKIE BOLIN, ROSIE BROWN, AND DARRYL DESS. (DAVID MCLANE, DAILY NEWS)

GIANTS' GIFFORD BACK AFTER YEAR'S LAYOFF

BY JOE O'DAY   APRIL 3, 1962

The Giffer is back and the Giants have him. Frank Gifford, a six-time All-Pro halfback, ended a one-year retirement yesterday by signing with the Eastern Division champs for an estimated $22,500.

A veteran of nine seasons, the 31-year-old recently severed his connections with a local radio station and decided to give the play-for-pay game another whirl.

"Retiring was a big mistake," Gifford declared. "There's still plenty of football left in me, I'm sure. Probably I'm not as strong as I was after laying off a year, but I'm at my old playing weight (196) and back in football as long as I can stay as a player."

One of the all-time great Giant halfbacks, Giff called it quits late in 1960 after being racked up by the Eagles' Chuck Bednarik at Yankee Stadium, Nov. 20. Although he suffered a concussion that hospitalized him for 12 days, Gifford denied the Bednarik incident influenced his retirement.

Coach Allie Sherman was enthusiastic about Gifford's comeback and said: "We're glad to have him back. We discussed this quite a bit before he made his decision, and we'll have to wait until we get into training camp before deciding how he'll fit into our three-end offense."

Asked about using Gifford at quarterback, Sherman added: "He won't be a quarterback, that's for sure. Frank will play at his strong positions, and we won't try to make a quarterback out of him."

During his nine-year tenure with the Maramen, Gifford set three club records—most points scored (370), most touchdowns (59), and most yards gained rushing (3,674)—and was named the league's Most Valuable Player in 1956, when the Giants won their last league championship by beating Chicago.

FRANK GIFFORD (LEFT), BACK WITH THE GIANTS AFTER HIS RETIREMENT OF ONE YEAR, POSES WITH COACH ALLIE SHERMAN, (MIDDLE) AND TEAM-MATE KYLE ROTE. (DAILY NEWS)

GIANTS 49-34 SKINS; Y.A. TIES TD PASS MARK

62,844 See 7 Air Shots As Tittle Hits 27 of 39

BY GENE WARD   **OCTOBER 29, 1962**

The Giants didn't just defeat the Redskins yesterday, they electrocuted the hapless and previously unbeaten Washingtonians with aerial fireworks by Y.A. Tittle, the likes of which even that old ace, Slingin' Sammy Baugh, never unleashed.

For two periods and half of another, this was an old-fashioned thriller such as these ancient rivals used to brew 25 years ago, but it wound up with the Giants winners, seven touchdowns to five (49-34), as Tittle tossed his way into the NFL record books with seven scoring pitches, covering 505 yards, to four assorted receivers.

A mob of 62,844—the third straight sellout in Yankee Stadium—watched their heroes break open what had been a tight, taut pitchers' duel between Tittle and young Norm Snead with a splurge of three third-period touchdowns. And when the hot-handed Tittle extended this flashy scoring streak to four in the sixth minute of the final period, the bloodthirsty clients still were shouting.

The Redskins had cut the Giant lead to 21-20 (the conversion after their second tally was blocked) on the initial play of the second half, as Snead completed an 80-yard aerial connection, longest of the game, with mercurial Bobby Mitchell. Then Tittle took to the airlines for the most sensational slinging in the history of Giant quarterbacking. When he cooled off, the Giants were on top, 49-20, and Yat, with seven aerial touchdowns, had equalled the record held jointly by Sid Luckman and Adrian Burk.

Moreover, he had snugged the Giants into Eastern Division second place with a 5-and-2 mark (to the Skins' 4-1-2).

QUARTERBACK Y.A. TITTLE SHOWS OFF THE FORM THAT LED TO SEVEN TOUCHDOWN THROWS AGAINST WASHINGTON. JOINING HIM AS FOOTBALL'S GREATEST AIR CIRCUS (LEFT TO RIGHT) ARE HUGH MCELHENNY, PHIL KING, DEL SHOFNER, AARON THOMAS, AND JOE WALTON. (DAILY NEWS)

GIANT WINDS BLOW NFL TITLE TO GREEN BAY

DECEMBER 31, 1962

Swirling winds and freezing temperatures grounded the Giants' vaunted passing attack and blew the NFL championship out of Yankee Stadium and back to Green Bay, Wisconsin. The mighty New Yorkers, champions of the Eastern Conference, lost yesterday's title battle with the Western Conference-champion Green Bay Packers, 16-7.

The day began cold, but calm. By game time, however, the temperatures had fallen to 19 degrees, with wind gusts of 40 miles per hour and a reported wind chill of minus-25 degrees. None of this kept the fans away, as 64,892 Giant backers crammed into Yankee Stadium to see the rematch of last year's NFL finalists.

But the cold and windy conditions thwarted the Giants' explosive aerial assault and turned this contest into ground war. After the game, Giant quarterback Y.A. Tittle explained that the swirling winds affected almost every pass (he completed just 18 of 41 throws), sometimes flying the ball into the stands and other times driving the ball into the frozen turf.

The Packers' ground attack led to an early 26-yard field goal, the only score in the first quarter. The Packers' second score occurred two plays after they recovered a New York fumble on the Giants' 28-yard line. A rare pass completion by the Packers and a seven-yard run by bruising Jim Taylor gave the visitors a 10-0 lead at halftime.

The Giants opened the scoring in the second half by blocking a Packer punt and recovering it in the end zone, cutting Green Bay's lead to 10-7. But the Giants' offense failed to muster any scoring on its own, and two second-half field goals by the Packers' Jerry Kramer provided the final margin, 16-7, keeping the NFL championship in Green Bay for another year.

Despite falling just short of the NFL championship prize, there was no questioning the grit and effort of this year's Giants. As Giant end Kyle Rote noted after the game, "I never saw a team that tried so hard and lost."

GIANTS QUARTERBACK Y.A. TITTLE ACCEPTS THE WEST SIDE ASSOCIA-
TION MOST VALUABLE PLAYER AWARD FOR LEADING HIS TEAM TO THE
1962 NFL TITLE GAME AGAINST GREEN BAY. (DAILY NEWS)

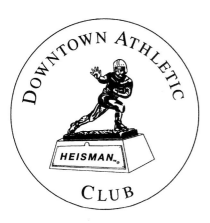

WINNING TRADITIONS...

*the
New York
Giants
and the
United States
Postal Service*

UNITED STATES POSTAL SERVICE®

A REAL GOOD JOE

Giants Rate Morrison Football's Greatest Utility Man

BY GENE WARD   **NOVEMBER 3, 1963**

Giants' quarterback Y.A. Tittle looked over the jammed, overloaded Minnesota Vikings' defense and decided upon calling the automatic. First looking to his left, then to his right, Tittle gave a quick glance over his shoulder and saw Joe Morrison—the National Football League's most complete player.

Shaking his head, Tittle quickly called time and grabbed Morrison by the shoulder, steering him all the time towards the Giants' bench. "Hell, the last time I looked, you were playing tight end. Before that it was the split. Man, I just can't keep up with you," Y.A. exploded.

Approaching the bench, Tittle yelled to coach Allie Sherman and added: "This guy's too much. I know you move him around, but give me a clue where he's supposed to be playing now."

Jocularly, Sherman looked at his veteran quarterback and roared: "Hell, he's playing fullback now and do me a favor and keep him away from the coaching line."

This, then, is Morrison, a rugged 26-year-old from Lima, Ohio, who in his short pro career (four years), has constantly confounded his teammates and opponents alike by playing a variety of offensive and defensive roles with equal agility and ability.

Sitting in his office recently at Yankee Stadium, Sherman puffed on a cigar and declared: "Joe's the closest thing we have to a utility man in football. I know they're a dime a dozen in baseball, but in this game it's entirely different. Lew Carpenter of the Packers and Dick James of the Redskins can handle any number of positions, but there's nobody, but nobody to compare with Joe all around. He's played the tight and split end, flanker, halfback, and fullback on offense in addition to running back kickoffs and punts. Also, we've used him on defense in the rough, strongside safety, where he handles the opposing tight end."

Line coach Ed Kolman agreed: "Every time I see him play, it just makes me feel good all over. I got real lucky with Joe."

OPPOSITE: JOE MORRISON'S TREMENDOUS VERSATILITY IS REFLECTED IN THE GIANTS' ALL-TIME STATISTICS, WHERE HE STANDS ATOP THE CAREER LIST IN RECEPTIONS (395), IS FIFTH IN TOTAL POINTS SCORED (390), AND TENTH IN RUSHING YARDS (2,472). (OSSIE LEVINESS, DAILY NEWS)

BEARS INTERCEPT NFL CROWN, 14-10

BY GENE WARD   DECEMBER 30, 1963

The Bears won their sixth NFL crown, 14-10, on the frigid tundra of Wrigley Field here yesterday afternoon as Y.A. Tittle turned into a very ordinary and mistake-prone aerialist.

In one of the sorriest showings of his career, the great Giant quarterback suffered five interceptions by the alert Bear defense, and two of them set the stage for the brace of touchdowns by Billy Wade which slapped the one-point-favored Easterners with their third straight championship defeat and their fifth in the last six years.

Tittle had an excuse, for he played the entire second half on a damaged left knee, the result of a twist as he slipped to the ground two-thirds of the way through the second quarter.

But it was scant consolation for the Giants, who had made such a gorgeous beginning as they slammed their way to a quick, first-quarter touchdown on a seven-play, two-pass sequence punctuated by the Bald Eagle's 14-yard TD pitch to his old reliable, Frank Gifford.

This was a glittering drive, the Giants making it look so easy that the partisan throng of 45,801 was silenced as though it had been doused with a huge pitcher of ice water on this 11-degree afternoon.

It was not enough, though, and Tittle's ailing knee got the best of him as Chicago went on to win, 14-10.

OPPOSITE: DESPITE A KNEE INJURY THAT TURNED GIANTS STAR Y. A. TITTLE INTO AN ORDINARY QUARTERBACK ON THIS DAY, TITTLE'S MUD-SOAKED BODY AND IRON WILL PUSHED THE GIANTS TO NEAR VICTORY IN THE 1963 NFL CHAMPIONSHIP GAME AGAINST THE CHICAGO BEARS. (DAILY NEWS)

EMLEN THE GREMLIN

BY GENE WARD   FEBRUARY 7, 1965

When Jack and Wellington Mara signed a young football player to a contract at the old Broad St. Station in Philadelphia on a hot August afternoon 16 years ago, little did they know what a prize they had captured.

His name was Emlen Tunnell, and he set the NFL on fire with his deeds of defensive derring-do.

The first black player for the Giants, he now is off and running for them again as the first of his race ever to win a coaching job in pro football. The contract he signed the other day as defensive coach does much to meet our flagging optimism concerning the Giants' chances for a comeback next season.

Emlen the Gremlin they used to call him because, like the fabled gremlins of WWII who played such havoc with aircraft, he had a penchant for fouling up aerial attacks. Four of the Giants' individual career records set by this main strut in Stout Steve Owen's famed "umbrella defense" still stand—most pass interceptions, 74; most yardage gained on interceptions, 1,240; most punt returns, 257; and most punt returns in a single season, 38.

Mild mannered and soft-spoken, he was harder than a keg of nails on the football field. He loved to smack down ballcarriers almost as much as he loved carrying the ball. He played 158 consecutive games, 126 of them (1948-58) with the Giants and the remainder with Green Bay.

As a defensive coach, his special assignment will be the reformation of a Giant secondary, which came apart at the seams last year. In addition to such veterans as Dick Lynch, Erich Barnes, Jimmy Patton, and Dick Pesonen, he has several 'hot' rookies to draw on in the remolding of the pass-defensive corps, a couple of them his discoveries.

The Giants will count themselves lucky if any one of them turns out to have half the talent of Emlen.

OPPOSITE: BESIDES BREAKING UP PASSES AS ONE OF THE PREMIER DEFENSIVE BACKS OF HIS TIME, EMLEN TUNNELL WAS RESPONSIBLE FOR BREAKING DOWN NFL BARRIERS. TUNNELL WAS THE FIRST BLACK PLAYER ON THE GIANTS, THE FIRST BLACK COACH IN ALL OF PRO FOOTBALL, AND THE FIRST BLACK MAN INDUCTED INTO THE PRO FOOTBALL HALL OF FAME. (DAILY NEWS)

THAT BIG KID ON THE GIANTS

BY FRANCIS M. STEPHENSON   NOVEMBER 7, 1965

"Football is football."

So spoke Tucker Frederickson, star rookie back of the New York Giants, when we asked him what difference he had found between pro ball and the collegiate game. He was All-America at Auburn.

And in this same direct style, this rugged 6-foot-3, 220-pound ball carrier has been hitting the line for hefty gains in his first year. He has a ready smile and speaks softly, but he is all business on the field. In early-season play, he showed up a surprising fourth in rushing in the NFL with a 3.9 average.

He has found the going rougher and tougher, but he is Coach Allie Sherman's No. 1 ball toter. And he was the Giants' No. 1 draft choice last winter.

And what do the Giants think of this rookie who has become their leading ground gainer? The man who knows—Coach Sherman—says:

"He does a lot of things well for a rookie. He has lots of ability and poise. Poise in a rookie is hard to come by. He is a real good driver, has good speed, wonderful balance, and he is a good blocker. He has a lot to learn. He will be a good player in his time."

That is rare praise from the usually tight-lipped Sherman.

Whatever may be the success of the Giants this season in their comprehensive rebuilding program, young Frederickson already has helped put them ahead of last year's disastrous 2-10-2 with an early 3-3 record. He seems a fixture destined for stardom in the brighter years ahead envisioned by Sherman.

Take the word of Dick Lynch, veteran Giants defensive back: "The first time I tackled him in scrimmage, I thought I had hit a truck."

OPPOSITE: AFTER BEING THE TOP PICK IN THE DRAFT AND EARNING ALL-PRO HONORS HIS ROOKIE SEASON, TUCKER FREDERICKSON (#24) SAW HIS CAREER FIZZLE AS A RESULT OF CHRONIC KNEE PROBLEMS. (ED CLARITY, DAILY NEWS)

THE GIANTS STILL PACK A .45

BY JERRY LISKER   OCTOBER 9, 1966

If I told you that Homer Jones' favorite movie is *Bambi* and that he didn't do any speaking on the grid banquet circuit last year because he never took "electrocution lessons," then, I guess you'd think you had a pretty clear picture of the Giants' pass-catching sensation.

The strapping 6-2, 210-pounder is rapidly reaching the point in his career where the "What, Me Worry?" image is evaporating and leadership qualities are beginning to bloom.

When the NFL issued its first statistics, one figure was an eye-opening whopper. Homer stood at the top of the pass-catching production list, averaging 86.5 yards a reception.

When activated in 1964, Homer was put on the kicking team and used sparingly at flanker. He took over the flanker post in 1965 when Frank Gifford retired, and caught fire. Homer snared 26 passes for 709 yards, which figures out to a phenomenal 27.3-yard percentage per catch! He scored six touchdowns, and his 89-yard TD reception on a toss from Earl Morrall was the longest scoring pass of the year in the loop.

Homer turned out to be just what the doctor ordered, as far as the Giants are concerned. Throughout their team history, the Maramen had always been crying loudly for the "bomb," the deep end who could break open a game with the long touchdown. Now they have him. Unfortunately, what they always had, they now lack, the tough running backs who doubled as strong blockers for such passers as Charlie Conerly and Y.A. Tittle, and the powerful up-front crews.

OPPOSITE: HOMER JONES TOPS THE GIANTS' RECORDS LIST FOR MOST RECEIVING YARDS GAINED IN A SEASON (1,209 IN 1967), HIGHEST AVERAGE RECEIVING GAIN IN A CAREER (22.6 YARDS), AND MOST RECEIVING TOUCHDOWNS IN A SEASON (13 IN 1967). (DAILY NEWS)

TUNNELL, STRONG JOIN PRO HALL

FEBRUARY 9, 1967

Ken Strong and Emlen Tunnell, heroes of separate eras when the New York Giants won championships in the National Football League, were among eight men who have been named to the National Pro Football Hall of Fame, officials announced yesterday.

Tunnell retired after the 1961 season, his 14th—11 with the Giants, the final three with the Green Bay Packers. He is the first player to enter the Hall of Fame primarily for his ability as a member of a defensive unit. Tunnell performed in the famous "umbrella" defensive backfield.

Tunnell also is the first black player to be selected in the five-year history of the nominations.

Now an assistant coach in charge of the Giant defensive backs, Tunnell holds four career NFL records—79 interceptions for 1,282 yards, 258 punt returns for 2,208 yards. He joined the Giants as a free agent when he walked into the club offices one day in 1948 and asked the late Tim Mara, then the owner, for a tryout.

Tunnell had played without much fanfare at Iowa and Toledo Universities. Strong, by comparison, had been an All-American halfback at New York University.

After starting his NFL career with the defunct Staten Island Stapletons in 1929, Ken Strong switched to the Giants in 1933. As a ball carrier, safety man, and placekicker, he scored 351 points, still the Giant record, before retiring at age 41 after the 1947 season.

OPPOSITE: GIANTS HALL OF FAMER KEN STRONG HAD ONE OF THE MOST VERSATILE GAMES IN ALL OF FOOTBALL. HIS PROWESS AS A KICKER, RUNNER, PASSER, AND DEFENDER LANDED HIM A SPOT ON THE PRO FOOTBALL HALL OF FAME'S ALL-NFL TEAM OF THE 1930S.

GIANTS TRADED "FUTURE" TO LAND TARKENTON FOR '67 COMEBACK

BY LARRY FOX   APRIL 2, 1967

The Giants, in what club president Wellington Mara called "our most expensive trade," recently obtained the colorful quarterback with whom they hope to counterattack not only the rest of the National Football League, but the image of the Jets' swinging Joe Namath.

He's Fran Tarkenton, at 27, a veteran of six years with the Vikings. A minister's son, he does own up to having a pool table in the basement of his Atlanta home.

A scrambler out of the U. of Georgia, Tarkenton shocked the Giants' brass by showing up at their offices wearing an olive-gold sports jacket, paisley tie, television blue shirt with a monogrammed cuff and tremendous green cuff links.

Namath belongs to the night people; Tarkenton is a member and director of the Fellowship of Christian Athletes. Unlike bachelor Joe, Tarkenton is married to his college sweetheart and has a two-year-old daughter—and has two good knees.

On the field he's an ultra-exciting heart-stopper and, considering what the Giants paid, he'd better be good. The price for the 6-foot, 195-pounder was the Giants' first- and second-round picks in the recent draft and their first selection next year, plus a player to be named later.

"To get quality, you've got to give up quality," head coach Allie Sherman added. "Fran is a fine pro quarterback whose ability, leadership, and experience will be a great asset to our young team."

OPPOSITE: THE NEW YORK GIANTS PINNED MANY OF THEIR HOPES ON FRAN TARKENTON WHEN THEY ACQUIRED HIM FROM THE MINNESOTA VIKINGS. (DAILY NEWS)

FRAN STEERS A GIANT-SIZED UPSET OF COWBOYS, 27-21

BY NORM MILLER   NOVEMBER 11, 1968

That CBS-TV spectacular which should have kept you riveted to the tube this afternoon was entitled "The Giants' Finest Hour." Actually, it wasn't an original script, just one never played before by this particular cast of characters, and it was a hands-down candidate for an Emmy Award.

The Giants' 27-21 win over the Dallas Cowboys in the windy setting of the Cotton Bowl was undoubtedly the most stunning upset under Allie Sherman's nine-year direction. It was something out of the Giants' glorious past and atoned for a multitude of sins of their more dismal recent seasons.

Suddenly now, the Giants are back in the Capitol Division race. This win by Sherman's 17 1/2-point underdogs leaves them 6-3; Dallas is 7-2. They meet again in New York in the final game of the season.

The shocker, before a partisan crowd of 72,163, was achieved on a variety of superlative contributions on this dark, overcast afternoon.

The most spectacular, of course, was the artistry of Fran Tarkenton and Homer Jones, co-starring for the first time in five games. There also was a gutty performance by the defense. The front line shut off the Cowboy running game with 99 yards, and the backfield, although leaky in the middle at times, made three big interceptions.

TACKLE & RECOVERY

PHOTO BY TOM WATSON, DAILY NEWS

Beattie Feathers of the Bears is tackled so strenuously by Tod Goodwin of the Giants that the ball slips out of his arms. It was recovered by Bob Bellinger of the Giants.

1940 STARTING LINEUP

PHOTO BY TOM WATSON, DAILY NEWS

The New York Giants' 1940 starting lineup: Front row, left to right: Jim Horneel, Gerry Dennerlien, John Dell Isola, captain Mel Hein, Orville Tuttle, Frank Cope, and Jim Poole. Back row, left to right: Ward Cuff, Walter Nielsen, Nello Falaschi, and Eddie Miller.

UMBRELLA DEFENSE

The backfield stalwarts of the Giants' famous umbrella defense in 1951 are (left to right) Harmon Rowe, Otto Schnellbacher, Emlen Tunnell, and Tom Landry.

STUDYING THE PLAYS

Giants football player Tom Landry studies plays with coaches Jim Lee Howell (left) and Vince Lombardi.

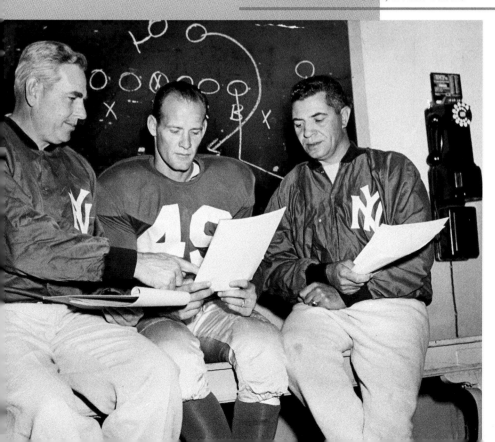

WHAT IF NEW YORK HAD A BRIDGE
THAT WENT ALL AROUND THE WORLD?

New York is home to hundreds of bridges. Including one that can take you just about

anywhere. It's the bridge called American Airlines®. And over 220* times every business day it

stretches from the New York area to Los Angeles, Chicago, London and hundreds of other

cities around the world. Call your Travel Agent or American at 1-800-433-7300. Or book online

at www.aa.com today. Getting where you want

to go is easy. As long as you take the right bridge.

AmericanAirlines
New York's Bridge To The World℠

member of oneworld

LOCKER ROOM CELEBRATION
PHOTO BY AP/WIDE WORLD PHOTOS

New York Giants quarterback Charlie Conerly, right, and teammate Frank Gifford celebrate in the locker room at Yankee Stadium in New York after crushing the Chicago Bears to win the National Football League championship on December 30, 1956.

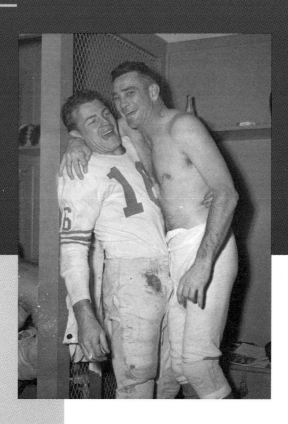

SUPER BOWL XXI
PHOTO BY KEITH TORRIE, DAILY NEWS

Giants head coach Bill Parcells is carried off the field by his players after winning Super Bowl XXI in Pasadena, California.

Tom Seaver
Hall of Fame Pitcher and
Chase Middle Market
Spokesperson

No matter how good you are... you need to know the team is behind you.

IN BASEBALL, BUSINESS AND BANKING, IT TAKES A TEAM TO REACH THE TOP.

More growing companies rely on Chase, the leading bank for business

Your Chase Relationship Manager heads a team of professionals dedicated exclusively to growing companies

As your guide and advocate, your Relationship Manager gives you access to credit, cash management, investments, leasing, merger and acquisition advice and financing, derivatives, international – a full range of products and services

We're the leading bank for business because, like you, we play hard. We play to win. And we love the game. Get the best team in banking for your business.

 CHASE

THE RIGHT RELATIONSHIP IS EVERYTHING.®

www.chase.com

1995 RETIRING PHIL SIMMS' NUMBER

Former Giants quarterback Phil Simms lifts his arms to the crowd after his number is retired by Giants president Wellington Mara, center, during halftime ceremonies at Giants Stadium on September 4, 1995.

1997 COACH OF THE YEAR HONORS

In his rookie year as the Giants' head coach, Jim Fassel earned 1997 Coach of the Year honors by leading New York to a 10-5-1 record atop the NFC East standings, including an undefeated 7-0-1 record in the division.

1997 HALL OF FAME INDUCTEE

PHOTO BY AP/WIDE WORLD PHOTOS

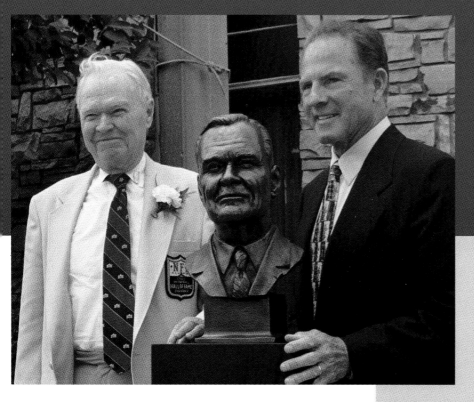

Wellington Mara, left, owner of the Giants, smiles alongside his Pro Football Hall of Fame bust, joined by his presenter, former New York Giants player Frank Gifford, after being inducted into the Pro Football Hall of Fame on July 26, 1997, in Canton, Ohio.

1999 PRO FOOTBALL HALL OF FAME

PHOTO BY AP/WIDE WORLD PHOTOS

New York Giants great Lawrence Taylor, right, is embraced by his son after Lawrence Jr. introduced him during enshrinement ceremonies at the Pro Football Hall of Fame on August 7, 1999.

FRAN TARKENTON'S ABILITY TO PERFORM UNDER PRESSURE LED THE GIANTS TO MANY DOWN-TO-THE-WIRE VICTORIES. (DAN FARRELL, DAILY NEWS)

GIANTS DRAFT DEFENSIVE END NO. 1

BY LARRY FOX   JANUARY 29, 1969

The Giants took themselves a sleeper in the first round of the draft, and only games will tell whether defensive end Fred Dryer of San Diego State is the 13th-best football prospect in the land.

Dryer, 6-6 and 230, is rated as a great pass rusher. He can do the 40 in 4.8 seconds and probably will play at 250. He's rated the best defensive end San Diego State ever had, including Leo Carroll, No. 1 pick of the Falcons two years ago.

Dryer said he had hoped to be drafted by a New York team, even though he has never even visited here. "I wasn't surprised to be drafted in the first round and I figure I can make any team," he said matter-of-factly.

For all his confidence, Dryer was a reluctant football player. In fact, he never played the game until his senior year in high school. "You know how impressionable you are then. Well, I never cared for football or sports, but all my friends were going out for football and so I went out, too," he recalled. "In junior college, I didn't go out for the team until my second year, and again because my friends were on the team. It was only then that I realized I might have a future in the game."

Dryer played two years at El Camino J.C. before moving on to San Diego State. His idol, not surprisingly, is Deacon Jones of the Rams.

OPPOSITE: ONCE A STANDOUT DEFENSIVE END FOR THE NEW YORK GIANTS, FRED DRYER HAS SINCE MADE A CAREER AS A TELEVISION STAR. (DAILY NEWS)

GIANTS STUN VIKINGS, 24-23

BY NORM MILLER   **SEPTEMBER 22, 1969**

It was just like the olden, golden days of the Giants, their incredible 24-23 come-from-behind win over the Vikings yesterday before 62,920 at Yankee Stadium — like many of the great games in which Alex Webster played for the old-champ Giants, like he has been saying he'd like it to be for the new Giants.

The Giants pulled out this first game in the new Webster Era with a pair of touchdowns in the final five minutes of the game, both from Fran Tarkenton to the rookie pass-catching phenom Don Herrmann, the game-winner coming with 59 seconds on the clock.

They pulled it out because Tarkenton shrugged off the booing of the crowd throughout a rough three periods, because the defense shone during the second half as it hasn't in the past five seasons, and because of a touch of luck, too, which generally comes to teams with unquenchable desire.

"Everyone laughed when I said Super Bowl the other day," Webster gloated in the clubhouse afterward. "It may be a long way, but it's possible. I don't think these kids know how really good they are. Nobody does."

Could you believe that from the time the Vikings took a 23-10 lead on Fred Cox's third field goal with 14 minutes left in the game, the Giants' defense did not allow a single first down?

Webster's contribution to this win was something more than inspiration. Midway through the final quarter, when the Giants were going nowhere against that tough Minny defensive front, the new coach made a vital decision.

"That front four was teeing off and coming at us," he explained.

"I said to Fran: 'Let's go to draws and quick screens.'"

This is usually the sound strategy against a strong defensive rush — provided the QB and his backs can execute. Tark and Tucker Frederickson, running as he didn't for Allie Sherman, pulled it off.

OPPOSITE: GIANTS QUARTERBACK FRAN TARKENTON (LEFT) AND DEFENSIVE END FRED DRYER CLOWN AROUND AFTER WINDING UP A HEAVY WORKOUT. (DAN FARRELL, DAILY NEWS)

WARD TO THE WISE

Giant Comeback Downs Redskins

BY GENE WARD   NOVEMBER 16, 1970

You had to be there to believe it . . . there in gloomy Yankee Stadium as the Giants, their glorious winning streak all but shattered, trailed the Redskins, 33-14, going into the final period. You had to see it with your own eyes to believe what the Giants did yesterday, as they turned disaster into triumph in a comeback which will be talked about as long as there are Giant fans.

The key to the magnificent comeback is contained in two words "to believe."

The Giants believe in themselves. Sitting beside his dressing cubicle in the locker room, the sweat still beading his face, Ron Johnson told it like it was to a solid, encircling ring of reporters and radio men.

Ron had scored the first of the Giants' three fourth-period touchdowns on a 5-yard burst up the gut of the Redskins' goal-line defense . . . and Ron had scored the winner on a 9-yard dash around the Redskins' right flank.

"How in the world," a man asked, "did a team three touchdowns behind ever dare to dream they could pull it out? How did you do it? Where did it come from?"

Ron Johnson thought a moment. "We got something from within," he said. "We believed."

Outside, on the dank ramps, as the fans flowed slowly toward the exits, one heard over and over again "unbelievable, absolutely unbelievable," this from tough Giant addicts who have seen almost everything over the years.

Inside, from one cubicle to another around the dressing room, you heard the same sermon, perhaps couched in different words, that Johnson was preaching—belief in themselves and in each other.

Fran Tarkenton had taken his offensive platoon, with Frederickson at fullback and Johnson at halfback, 86 yards, including 15 yards for offensive interference, for a touchdown at 5:19 of the fourth period, slicing the Redskins' lead to 33-21. At 7:04 of the fourth period, Tarkenton had completed a 57-yard touchdown connection with Frederickson, slicing the Redskins' lead to 33-28.

And, with one minute left to play, Tarkenton had handed off to Johnson, who ran 9 yards around the Redskins' right flank, making the Giants the winners, 35-33.

"This is a team which believes in itself," Tarkenton said. "We believe in each other."

A JUBILANT RON JOHNSON (#30), CELEBRATES THE GAME-WINNING TOUCH-
DOWN WITH A MINUTE LEFT TO BEAT THE REDSKINS, 35-33. LATER IN THE SEA-
SON, JOHNSON BECAME THE FIRST GIANT EVER TO BREAK THE 1,000-YARD
RUSHING MARK. JOHNSON FINISHED THE SEASON WITH 1,027 YARDS RUSHING.
(FRANK HURLEY, DAILY NEWS)

ROBUSTELLI, TITTLE JOIN VINCE IN HALL OF FAME

BY LARRY FOX   FEBRUARY 5, 1971

The archives list their achievements, but to Wellington Mara, president of the Giants and son of a Hall of Famer, the new Pro Football Hall of Famers are live men. Two, Y.A. Tittle and Andy Robustelli, played for the Giants. Vince Lombardi was an assistant coach. Fellow inductees Norm Van Brocklin, Jim Brown, Bruiser Kinard, and Bill Hewitt were respected opponents.

Two of the inductees, Tittle and Robustelli, enjoyed their greatest days with the Giants after beginning their careers elsewhere.

Tittle, originally in the old All-American Conference, played for a decade with the 49ers, who shipped him off to the Giants before the 1961 season in exchange for lineman Lou Cordileone. Believed to be washed up, Tittle still had enough to direct the Giants to three championships. Robustelli, an outstanding defensive end, started his 14-year pro career with the Rams before coming to New York in another of the Giants' great deals. "The most completely competitive guy that I can remember ever being with us. There's no question that Andy put us over the top in 1956," said Wellington Mara.

Lombardi, a native of Brooklyn, first came to pro coaching as an assistant with the Giants. He went to Green Bay as head coach in 1960 and took a floundering franchise to five NFL championships and two straight Super Bowl victories.

OPPOSITE: DURING HIS HALL OF FAME CAREER, ANDY ROBUSTELLI PLAYED IN SEVEN PRO BOWLS AND EIGHT NFL CHAMPIONSHIP GAMES, INCLUDING THE GIANTS' 1956 TITLE MATCH. HIS DURABILITY WAS ALSO LEGENDARY—HE MISSED ONLY ONE GAME IN 14 SEASONS. (DAILY NEWS)

GRID GIANTS SIGN FOR JERSEY BOUNCE

BY LARRY FOX   AUGUST 27, 1971

The football Giants bought their bus ticket to Jersey yesterday, signing a 30-year lease to start play in the proposed 75,000-seat Giants Stadium in the Hackensack Meadows no later that 1975.

The theme of the joint announcement made at the Essex House by Jersey Gov. William T. Cahill, Giants president Wellington Mara, and David A. (Sonny) Werblin, chairman of the New Jersey Sports and Exposition Authority, was: "We're moving, but we're not leaving," and Mara insisted that his team would not change its name.

"We are and we always intend to be the New York football Giants," he declared.

The new stadium, part of a proposed sport complex, will be built in East Rutherford, about 6 to 8 miles northwest of the Lincoln Tunnel. It will cost $10 million, according to the governor.

Cahill said he hoped that construction could begin "by the end of the year," but he said nothing could be done on the sale of bonds to finance the project until the complex, including a race track, were approved by the courts.

Cahill called the signing "a great day for the state of New Jersey, the fans of the New York Giants, and for all the citizens of New York."

Mara pointed to the Giants' history of 31 years in the Polo Grounds and then the last 15 seasons, also as tenants of a baseball team, in Yankee Stadium.

Each stadium was the most famous of its era, but every family dreams of the day it can move into its own home and go away from its in-laws, no matter how great the relatives have been to live with . . . and our relations with the Yankees have been great," Mara said.

Mara said his prime consideration in making the move was "our duty to our fans."

"If you have a seat at Yankee Stadium, you will have a better one in Giants Stadium, and 10,000 to 15,000 of you who don't have seats in Yankee Stadium will have one in Giants Stadium," Mara said.

JOHN MARA (RIGHT), PRESIDENT OF THE NEW YORK GIANTS, HOLDS A
FOOTBALL OVER A PICTURE OF YANKEE STADIUM. AFTER 17 YEARS OF
PLAYING THERE, THE GIANTS WILL MOVE ON TO THE YALE BOWL AND
SHEA STADIUM, BEFORE SETTLING AT GIANTS STADIUM IN 1976. (DAILY
NEWS)

GIANTS MANGLE EAGLES, 62-10, REGISTER SCORING MARK

BY NORM MILLER   NOVEMBER 27, 1972

It may come as a surprise to Giant fans rejoicing over the record 62-10 shellacking of the poor Eagles at Yankee Stadium yesterday afternoon that this humiliation was an embarrassment to Alex Webster.

Many of the late-stayers among the 62,586 who cheered this wildest scoring binge in the Giants' 48-year history may have noticed Webster chewing out Randy Johnson for, let's say, overzealousness beyond the code of discretion in such matters.

This victory total, which topped a 56-0 clobbering of the Eagles back in 1933, also was the highest of the year in the NFL. It left the Giants with a 7-4 record, one game behind the runner-up Cowboys in the NFC chase for the wild card playoff spot.

The luckiest thing that happened to the Eagles yesterday was that this drubbing was not televised back to the Philadelphia area because of the CBS technicians' strike.

Philly set up 27 of the Giants' first 48 points with three lost fumbles and two interceptions against John Reaves, their rookie quarterback. The Giants led, 24-3, before 18 minutes had elapsed and 38-10 at halftime.

They also amassed 503 yards, out-first-downed the Eagles, 28-8, controlled the ball for 41 of the 60 minutes, and ran off 73 plays to Philadelphia's 43.

As for the individual accomplishments:

Ron Johnson gained 123 yards in 22 rushes to come within 53 of the 1,000-yard mark. He scored twice, once on a great 35-yard run.

Norm Snead threw three touchdown passes in a 9-for-16, 105-yard afternoon. Two of these were beauts of 15 and 29 yards.

And after Randy Johnson took over at quarterback with less than four minutes to play in the third quarter, he hooked up for two TD passes with Don Herrmann.

THE HIGH-SCORING 1972 GIANTS WERE LED BY NEWLY ACQUIRED QUARTERBACK NORM SNEAD (#16), WHO JOINED THE TEAM IN THE FRAN TARKENTON TRADE TO MINNESOTA. SNEAD'S LEAGUE-LEADING PASSING DROVE THE GIANTS TO A WINNING SEASON (8-6) FOR ONLY THE SECOND TIME IN NINE YEARS. (GENE KAPPOCK, DAILY NEWS)

HOW LONG CAN GIANTS FANS WAIT FOR REVIVAL?

BY NORM MILLER   **DECEMBER 9, 1975**

As the elevator at Shea descended from mezzanine to ground floor level Sunday with its assorted cargo of paying customers heading home and newsmen bound for the losing Giants' dressing room, the voice of a boy of about 15 spoke up: "I've always been a good Giant fan," he piped to the elders at his side, "but how long can I wait?"

"You have a long life ahead of you, son," replied Andy Robustelli, the Giants' GM also heading for the clubhouse, in a message he no doubt would convey to all such unhappy Giant fans these days.

True, Andy, during the lifetime of that youngster, the Giants inevitably will improve, as other clubs have, and maybe even someday play in the Super Bowl.

The questions of the moment, however, are how long are Giant fans willing to wait, and how long is boss Wellington Mara willing to wait, and how long can coach Bill Arnsparger AFFORD to wait for something encouraging to happen to this ballclub that is now 3-9?

It is now nearly two years since Mara phased himself out of the direct operation of the Giants and turned the job over to "professionals." If there has been any progress, it's been hard to discern. There was a high spot in the Monday night win over the Bills and now five straight losses.

"We'll grow up someday," Arnsparger promises of the squad of predominantly young Giants in whom he is staking the future.

The haunting question from the kid in the elevator comes back: "How long can I wait?"

"I am pleased with the progress we (the players) are making as individuals," Arnsparger says, "but we just don't have it yet as a team to do the things it takes to win."

And again the kid's question, "How long can I wait?"

Next year, it would seem, would be crisis season for this regime. There will be heat on the brass to draft well, heat on the coaches to develop talent, and heat on the players to produce.

And if they don't, it'll be a tossup to speculate on whether it's Wellington Mara or the fans who first say, "Hey, I can't wait any longer."

THE QUESTION ON EVERYONE'S MIND WAS THE SAME, "HOW LONG BEFORE THE GIANTS ARE GOOD AGAIN?" UNTIL THEN, THE FANS CONTINUED TO DISPLAY THEIR UNHAPPINESS WITH GIANTS MANAGEMENT. (MEL FINKELSTEIN, DAILY NEWS)

GIANTS PLAY IN FIRST GAME AT MEADOWLANDS

24-14 Opening Loss to Cowboys

BY NORM MILLER   OCTOBER 11, 1976

A large banner held aloft by a fan immediately after the Cowboys had driven 65 yards to their first touchdown with the game less than seven minutes old told the story of the Giants' housewarming flop yesterday: "BRAND NEW STADIUM, SAME OLD GIANTS."

Neither the inspiration from their beautiful new home, nor the 76,042 who came to cheer, nor a reminder of glories past could bail out the party. The 24-14 setback by the Cowboys was strictly a bummer.

"The fans were ready to play today," coach Bill Arnsparger commented with a twinge of irony. It's true, the SRO crowd was aching for heroics to cheer. Instead, they wound up booing the kind of mistakes now becoming monotonous.

The setback dropped the Giants' record to 0-5, the poorest season start in the 52-year history of the franchise.

Among the disappointed were six members of the very first Giant team of 1925 and the greater portion of their last championship club of '56.

Snead's 4-for-4 passing in moving the Giants 86 yards in the late minutes, and two tremendous catches by 5-9, 170-pound Jimmy Robinson, were just about the only bright Giant moments in this fifth straight Cowboy win.

WHILE THE GIANTS' NEW HOME IN THE MEADOWLANDS WAS UNDER CONSTRUCTION, THE TEAM PLAYED ITS 1975 HOME SCHEDULE AT SHEA STADIUM AND THE FIRST FOUR GAMES OF THE 1976 SEASON ON THE ROAD. WHEN THEY FINALLY ARRIVED IN THEIR NEW STADIUM, THE GIANTS DROPPED THEIR FIRST THREE HOME GAMES. BUT THEY REBOUNDED WITH WINS IN THREE OF THEIR LAST FOUR HOME GAMES. (PAT CARROLL, DAILY NEWS)

GIFFORD GAINS GRID HALL

BY LARRY FOX   JANUARY 18, 1977

Gale Sayers, Forrest Gregg, and Bart Starr were swept into the Pro Football Hall of Fame in their first year of eligibility as part of a five-member class of '77 announced here yesterday that also included Frank Gifford and Bill Willis.

Gifford, a 12-year standout for the Giants as runner, receiver, and defensive back, had begun to wonder whether his time ever would come. A player must be out of the game for five years before he is eligible for enshrinement, and Gifford had been waiting for six years beyond that.

"I was certainly aware that it (election) might not happen," Gifford said yesterday. "Players are so much better today. Each year they're better than the year before, and as you move down the line, you know there are others who will be more seriously considered. I never resented anyone who went in before me, but I knew there was a good possibility that it wouldn't happen."

At a morning press conference, Gifford reminisced about a past Pro Bowl.

"It was 1953, I think, in Los Angeles, and that's where the players' union was formed. I was a charter member," he recalled. "Kyle Rote represented the Giants and I was with Kyle. I remember we did it surreptitiously because we didn't know if football was ready to accept the idea of a union. In fact, I thought it was all a joke and I thought we ought to get our fannies out of there before we got into a lot of trouble."

Gifford remembered that the Giant team's first "demand" was for $10 a week "laundry money" during training, and he pointed out that it was five or six more years before the union was recognized.

OPPOSITE: AMONG FRANK GIFFORD'S MANY HALL OF FAME ACHIEVEMENTS, HE STANDS ATOP THE GIANTS' ALL-TIME LISTS FOR CAREER TOUCHDOWNS (78), MOST RECEIVING YARDS (5,434), AND MOST CONSECUTIVE GAMES SCORING TOUCHDOWNS (10). (DAILY NEWS)

LAST-SECOND FUMBLE

BY NORM MILLER   NOVEMBER 20, 1978

Of all the excruciating games the Giants have blown down through their last decade and a half of misery, probably none could top yesterday's 19-17 loss to the Eagles.

It was the kind of crusher that could cost a coach his job.

Leading by five points with 32 seconds left to play and the Eagles out of timeouts, the Giants blew it all on a debatable call by the offensive braintrust and a murderous fumble by Joe Pisarcik.

It was as simple as this: all they needed to do was have Pisarcik take the center snap and fall to the ground with several brawny linemen standing by to protect him, as you've seen QB's do many, many times to kill the clock.

Instead, the braintrust called for a handoff to Larry Csonka and a plunge into the line. When the play came in from the sidelines, most of the offensive unit, Pisarcik included, questioned it.

What followed was a thousand-to-one shot for any gambler. As Pisarcik pivoted to his left with the snap, his handoff hit Csonka on the hip and fell free at the New York 26-yard line. Pisarcik made a dive for it, but Eagle cornerback Herman Edwards beat him to the source.

Edwards scooped up the fumble and ran it into the end zone untouched for the winning touchdown with 20 seconds remaining.

"This is the most horrifying ending to a ballgame I've ever seen," said a crushed John McVay.

OPPOSITE: WHILE ALL GIANTS FAN WOULD LIKE TO ERASE THIS FINISH FROM THEIR MEMORIES, IT REMAINS ONE OF THE MOST TALKED ABOUT MOMENTS IN RECENT TEAM HISTORY. (AP/WIDE WORLD PHOTOS)

DOLPHIN SUPER SCOUT YOUNG TAKES POST

BY BILL MADDEN   **FEBRUARY 15, 1979**

The war between the Maras came to an abrupt truce last night when the Giants' co-owners plucked George Young from the Dolphins organization as the surprise choice to run their football operations.

The selection of the 48-year-old Young, who was given a five-year contract and the title of general manager, ended an exhaustive 58-day search that brought into the open the long- simmering strife between Giants' president Wellington Mara and his nephew, Tim.

However, both Maras, who share the ownership of the Giants, insisted Young was a choice they agreed upon.

"His name came up when we were exploring names to fill our coaching vacancy," Tim Mara said. "We both agreed we should talk to him."

The surprise announcement of Young came after the Maras met all day with NFL Commissioner Pete Rozelle in the league offices.

That was Tuesday. Yesterday morning, Young was on a plane to New York and, at approximately 4 p.m., he was offered the job of refurbishing the Giant franchise from its present chaotic condition.

Naturally, Young's first order of business will be to select a coach to replace John McVay.

"Inasmuch as I was only contacted yesterday, I haven't had any time to think about that," Young said. "However, I realize we have to name a coach as soon as possible. But haste is not going to make this decision, being rational will. I want to look over all the possible candidates and meet with them before I make any decision.

Wellington Mara assured Young he would have a free hand in making that decision.

THE REBIRTH OF THE GIANTS' WINNING TRADITION TOOK OFF AFTER THE HIRING OF NEW GENERAL MANAGER GEORGE YOUNG. YOUNG BROUGHT IN HEAD COACHES RAY PERKINS AND BILL PARCELLS AND WAS RESPONSIBLE FOR THE DRAFTS THAT LANDED PHIL SIMMS, LAWRENCE TAYLOR, JOE MORRIS, CARL BANKS, MARK BAVARO, AND RODNEY HAMPTON. (GENE KAPPOCK, DAILY NEWS)

PHIL SIMMS: HE LIKES TO THROW

BY LARRY FOX   MAY 4, 1979

Who is Phil Simms? Well, the scouts at least know about the Giants' new quarterback. As long ago as last spring, the Moorehead State passer was listed as one of the sleepers for the 1979 draft by the Jets' personnel department in its annual exclusive preview for the *Daily News*.

So how come this sleeper stayed asleep? Simms explains that for his senior season, Moorehead's coach elected to ignore his quarterback's proven passing skills to put in a ball-control offense. Simms spent most of the time handing off, and at year's end, didn't even make the Ohio Valley Conference all-star team.

"I didn't particularly like it," Simms said of the new offense. Neither did anyone else connected with the school. Moorehead slumped to a 2-6-1 record and the coach was fired.

"I like the throwing part," Simms said yesterday after being drafted by the Giants. "I prefer putting it up 35 times a game."

Simms says he was also a sleeper coming out of high school, which is why he ended up at Moorehead. He's 6-2, 216 now, but four years ago, he weighed only 175 pounds.

Simms, a history major who will graduate on schedule in June, says he never dreamed he would be a first-round choice, projecting himself high on the second cycle. "Everybody was saying, 'He's a good quarterback, but he plays for Moorehead.'"

Simms, who says his main strength is an ability to "stay in the pocket against a heavy rush" as a drop-back passer, is in the middle of an athletic family that includes seven children.

OPPOSITE: GIANTS COACH RAY PERKINS AND HIS NEWEST QUARTERBACK, PHIL SIMMS, GET ACQUAINTED AT GIANTS STADIUM. (DAILY NEWS)

GIANTS TO SIGN TAYLOR

BY GARY MYERS   MAY 28, 1981

Lawrence Taylor, the North Carolina linebacker the Giants made their No. 1 pick with the second selection in last month's draft, will sign a three-year, $900,000 contract with the team during this week's mini-camp, the *Daily News* learned Wednesday.

"It's a superior contract," said a source close to the negotiations. "It's a lot better than the one Lam Jones signed with the Jets last year."

Taylor, who will easily become the highest-paid Giant and the first of the 1981 first-round picks to sign, will receive $500,000 in salary over the three years. He'll also get a $100,000 signing bonus and a tax-free, interest-free $300,000 loan from the Giants which is payable in the year 2025. If invested conservatively, the loan could be worth many times the $300,000 by the time it comes due.

Taylor took out a 60-day insurance policy with Lloyds of London, guarding against injury during the three-day minicamp, which starts Thursday at Giants Stadium, until he actually puts his name on the contract.

Giants general manager George Young was in Los Angeles last week, meeting with Taylor's agent, Mike Trope, where they worked out the details. Young has a stubborn policy of downplaying individual signings and Wednesday refused comment on the contracts of his top two picks.

OPPOSITE: THE DRAFTING OF LAWRENCE TAYLOR PAID IMMEDIATE DIVIDENDS. THE GIANTS WENT 9-7 DURING TAYLOR'S ROOKIE SEASON AND MADE THE NFL PLAYOFFS FOR THE FIRST TIME SINCE 1963. TAYLOR EARNED PRO BOWL HONORS, WAS NAMED TO THE ALL-NFL TEAM, AND RECEIVED THE DOUBLE HONOR OF NFL DEFENSIVE ROOKIE OF THE YEAR AND DEFENSIVE PLAYER OF THE YEAR. (KEITH TORRIE, DAILY NEWS)

ROB LEFT, ROB RIGHT, AND GIANTS ROB EAGLES

BY MIKE LUPICA   DECEMBER 28, 1981

Carpenter's Giants— and they were every bit his Giants yesterday—got three touchdown passes from Scott Brunner in their 27-21 victory over the Eagles, and they got big breaks, and they got defense, because these gritty, dreaming Giants always give you defense.

But on the day when they proved just how much they belong in Parity Rozelle's playoffs, what the Giants did was Rob the Eagles. Capitalize the verb. Rob as in Carpenter. Rob left, and Rob right, and Rob up the middle, every time the Giants needed the yards that were going to fuel a trip to San Francisco.

Carpenter gained 161 yards on 33 carries against an Eagle defense that was the best in the NFL this season in total yards allowed and total points allowed. The longest gain was 21 yards, which meant that he bled those yards out of the Eagles, again and again, when they knew he was going to carry the football. The Giants ran 57 offensive plays in the game; Carpenter was involved in 37, because he also caught four passes.

At one point in the second half, Carpenter carried the ball for the Giants on 13 straight offensive plays, and 17 of 18. Until Scott Brunner started falling on the football at the end, with the clock running down, and his teammates having a high-five festival on the sidelines, Carpenter had been involved in all but one play in the second half. Try to remember all the days across all the years when a Giant running back played a game quite like this.

And now, in the locker room, someone asked Rob Carpenter if he was tired. He smiled the hero's smile again.

"These are the playoffs," he said. "I'd be running out there right now if I had to be."

"He just kept asking for the ball," said Brunner, whose three touchdown passes gave the Giants the 27-7 halftime lead. "And we just kept giving it to him."

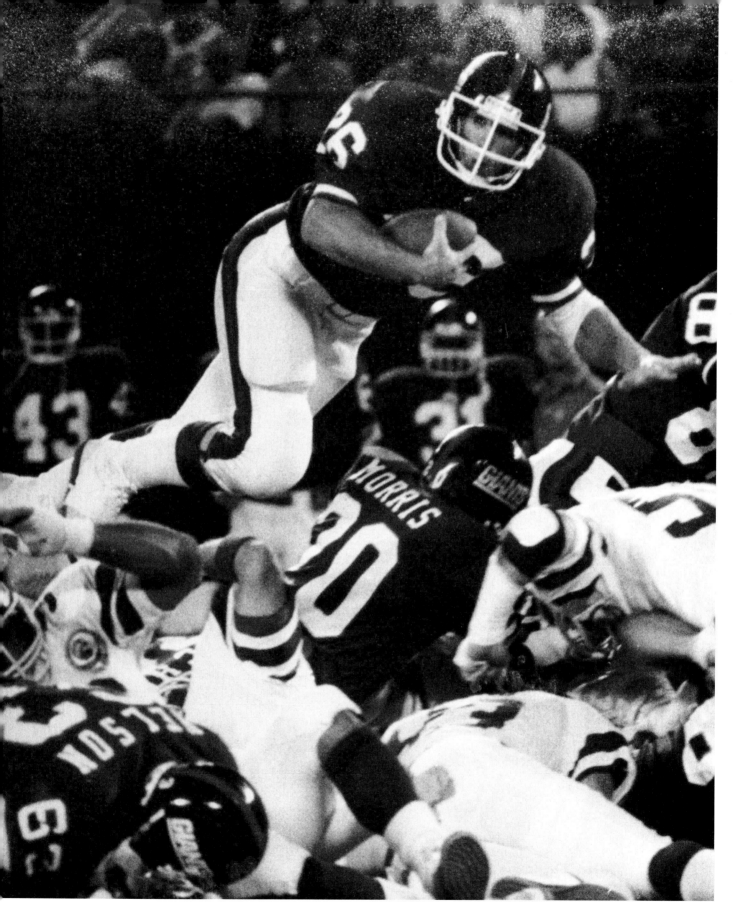

ROB CARPENTER'S 161 YARDS RUSHING AND SCOTT BRUNNER'S
THREE TOUCHDOWN PASSES LED THE GIANTS TO THEIR FIRST
POSTSEASON VICTORY IN MORE THAN TWO DECADES. (BILL STAHL,
DAILY NEWS)

SAM HUFF FINALLY MAKES IT

Hall of Fame Becomes Part of His Violent World

BY JOE O'DAY   JANUARY 29, 1982

This weekend Sam Huff will again be in the Hawaiian Islands—the island of Oahu to be exact—where the ex-Giants' and Redskins' linebacker will "officially" be notified of his election to the Pro Football Hall of Fame on the eve of the Pro Bowl Game in Aloha Stadium, Honolulu.

The 47-year-old, who is remembered by latter-day Giant fans as a winner in those OTB commercials, often asked— as recently as two months ago — why he wasn't considered for the Hall.

Joe Schmidt of the Lions and the Bears' Bill George were Atilla the Hun reincarnate in their time along with Huff.

"How come I was compared with them?" Huff asked in a recent Flashback in the *Sunday News*, November 29, 1981. "They're in the Hall of Fame and I'm not."

Say it no more, Sam. The electors, one from each franchise city in the National Football League, corrected the injustice on the eve of Super Bowl XVI in Dearborn, Michigan, when No. 70 was tabbed for immortality along with three others, who will be named tomorrow. Huff, who was drafted as an offensive guard and tackle following an outstanding career at West Virginia, was turned into a linebacker by then-defensive coach Tom Landry. As a rookie, the 6-1, 230-pounder was part of the Giants' last championship team in 1956, when they beat the Bears, 47-7.

Huff, who was the NFL's Outstanding Lineman in 1959 and the Pro Bowl's MVP in 1961, feels the game was more "violent" or "physical" in his time.

"The rules have been changed drastically for the offense," he recalled. "Then, too, the game is too specialized. I think fans like that physicalness . . . it should be part of the game."

OPPOSITE: THROUGHOUT HIS OUTSTANDING CAREER, SAM HUFF PLAYED IN FIVE PRO BOWLS AND SIX NFL CHAMPION-SHIP GAMES AND WAS THE 1959 NFL LINEMAN OF THE YEAR. (DAILY NEWS)

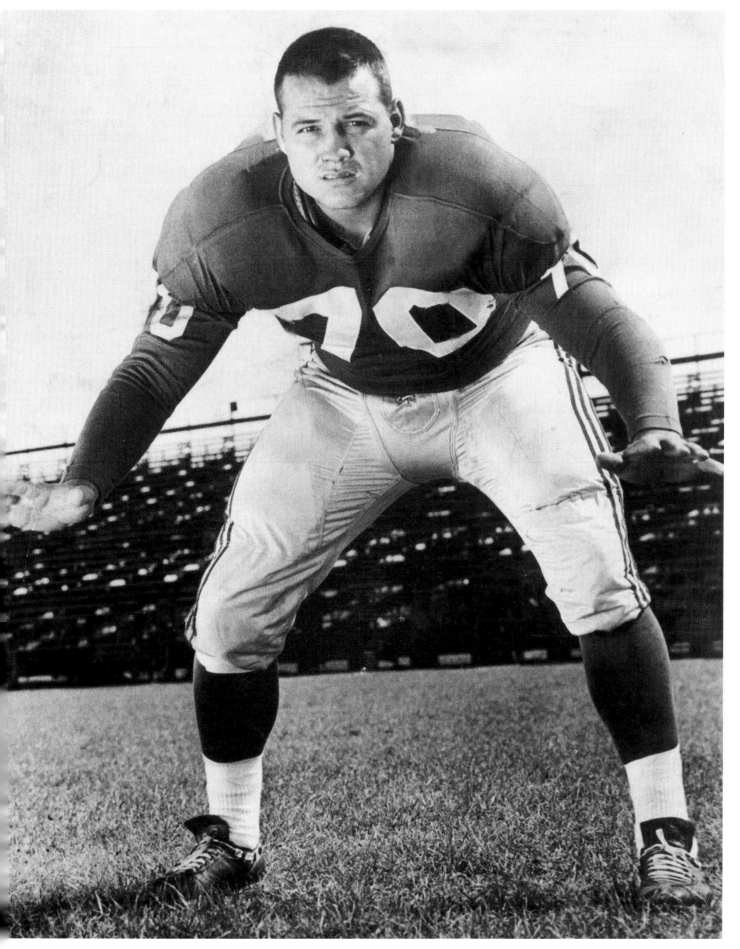

TAYLOR-MADE GIANT VICTORY

Linebacker's Big Play Stops Bucs, 17-14

BY BILL VERIGAN   SEPTEMBER 24, 1984

The Giants won this one with mirrors and Lawrence Taylor. Their 3-1 record might be an illusion that will shatter, but Taylor was very real yesterday as the Giants defeated the Tampa Bay Bucs, 17-14, at Giants Stadium.

Taylor was the Giants yesterday as they pushed off to their best four-game start since 1968.

The running game went nowhere. The receivers dropped five passes. Even Ali Haji-Sheikh missed another field goal, his third in four tries.

But the Bucs were wiped out by Taylor. He had four sacks. He forced a fumble and an interception. The first turnover led to a touchdown three plays later, the second eventually accounted for field position that provided the other touchdown.

Without him, it's hard to imagine that the Giants would have defeated the Bucs. With him, they barely won.

"Our whole game plan was designed to stop him," said Steve DeBerg, the Tampa Bay quarterback. "He was awesome. He created total chaos for our entire offense."

Taylor turns best-laid plans into mislaid plans or misplayed plans. He put this one through a shredder.

"I thought they were using deception," he said. "I was coming in so wide open, I thought they were trying to trick me. I came from a couple of different areas, and every one was pretty open."

OPPOSITE: LAWRENCE TAYLOR AND GIANTS COACH BILL PARCELLS TALK DEFENSE AT THE TEAM'S PRACTICE. OF HIS STAR PLAYER, PARCELLS SAID, "HE'S THE GREATEST PLAYER I EVER COACHED." (KEITH TORRIE, DAILY NEWS)

WELLINGTON'S ALWAYS THERE

BY BILL VERIGAN   DECEMBER 12, 1984

The biography of the Giants' president, Wellington Mara, takes up the middle of one sentence, almost as an afterthought near the bottom of page 15 of the teams' 1984 media guide.

"From the commencement of that Mara family ownership and tradition in 1925 with Tim Mara, it has continued unbroken and undaunted down through the decades with Tim's sons, the late John V. Mara, who served as president of the club until his death in 1965, and to Wellington T. Mara, who has been president since Jack's death, to Tim Mara II, Jack's son, who is now vice president and treasurer."

That's it. There's not even a picture. Leon Hess gets an entire page in the Jets' guide. So does Donald Trump in the Generals' guide.

"We just never got around to saying more, said the 68-year-old Mara. If you want to know more, come by Giants Stadium almost any day. While the team practices, he walks briskly around the field in an old, basic gray sweat suit and keeps his eyes on the field.

After games, he passes through the locker room, sticking out his hand to the players, patting them on the shoulder.

When they lost, he suffered with them. People who say he was consoled by the sellouts know nothing of the man. He waited longer than anyone for a return to glory.

For the last four seasons (excluding 1983, which was as dreadful as any within memory), the Giants have been on the brink. In 1981, they actually reached the playoffs, and now they are on the verge of going again.

"I'd be very disappointed if we don't make the playoffs," he said. "That's an emotion. But I reasonably understand that we've been better than almost anybody's expectations. It's very gratifying to see the improvement after all the hard work."

CLAD IN HIS USUAL
BASIC GRAY SWEAT
SUIT, GIANTS PRESI-
DENT WELLINGTON
MARA WAS FRE-
QUENTLY PRESENT AT
GIANTS PRACTICES TO
OBSERVE HIS TEAM.
MARA, WHO WAS EN-
SHRINED IN THE PRO
FOOTBALL HALL OF
FAME IN 1997,
JOINED HIS FATHER,
TIM (A 1963 CHARTER
ENSHRINEE), AS THE
ONLY FATHER AND
SON HONORED IN THE
HALL OF FAME.
(HARRY HAMBURG,
DAILY NEWS)

MASTERY, MISERY FOR SIMMS

Passes for 513 Yards

BY BILL VERIGAN   OCTOBER 14, 1985

The guy who said "statistics are for losers" should have seen the Giants' 35-30 loss to be Cincinnati Bengals yesterday.

While quarterback Phil Simms was setting all kinds of passing records, the Giants were setting unofficial records for futility.

Simms shattered three club records in completing 40-of-62 passes for 513 yards, and the defense allowed minus-three yards in the second half and a total of 199 in the game. But when it was over, the Giants had suffered their second straight loss and dropped to 3-3, while the Bengals had raised their season record to 2-4.

Simms' yardage total surpassed the 505 recorded by Y.A. Tittle vs. Washington, October 28, 1962. In fact, Simms turned in the second-most productive passing performance in NFL history, topped only by the 554 yards amassed by Ram quarterback Norm Van Brocklin vs. the New York Yankees in 1951. Simms' attempts and completions surpassed the 36-for-53 club-record performance of Charlie Conerly vs. Pittsburgh, December 5, 1948.

SIMMS IN THE RECORD BOOK

PHIL SIMMS ENTERED INTO SOME ELITE COMPANY WITH HIS BIG PASSING DAY. THE GIANT QUARTERBACK'S 513 YARDS ARE THE SECOND MOST IN NFL HISTORY. HERE ARE THE TOP SINGLE-DAY PERFORMANCES:

1. 554, NORM VAN BROCKLIN, L.A. VS. N.Y. YANKEES, SEPTEMBER 28, 1951
2. 513, PHIL SIMMS, N.Y. GIANTS VS. CINCINNATI BENGALS, OCTOBER 13, 1985
3. 509, VINCE FERRAGAMO, L.A. RAMS VS. CHICAGO, DECEMBER 26, 1982
4. 505, Y.A. TITTLE, N.Y. GIANTS VS. WASHINGTON, OCTOBER 28, 1962
5. 496, JOE NAMATH, N.Y. JETS VS. BALTIMORE, SEPTEMBER 24, 1972

IN ADDITION TO HIS RECORD-SETTING 513-YARD DAY AGAINST
CINCINNATI, PHIL SIMMS HOLDS ALMOST EVERY MEANINGFUL
RECORD FOR A GIANTS QUARTERBACK. (KEITH TORRIE, DAILY
NEWS)

TAYLOR HIT MAY DRAW CURTAIN ON THEISMANN

BY MIKE LUPICA   NOVEMBER 19, 1985

It was supposed to be a trick play. Gadget play. Washington quarterback Joe Theismann handed the ball off to John Riggins. Receivers streaked down the right sideline and down the middle and fooled no one in the Giants' secondary. Riggins pitched the ball back to Theismann. He looked down the field. Nothing. And now the world started to close in on him.

Theismann stepped up in the pocket. Harry Carson was there. Theismann, looking like the escape artist he has always been, wriggled away from Carson. Taylor came next. Lawrence Taylor. LT.

Theismann tried to fold himself up into the fetal position, just take the hit. And it seemed he had done that. But his left leg moved and his right leg did not. On the replay you could see Theismann's right leg bend in this terrible way, all wrong, and then disappear underneath him and Lawrence Taylor.

Theismann did not get up. The doctors came out and the trainer and Taylor stayed there, because LT knew it was bad. The stretcher came finally. It was quiet in RFK Stadium. Theismann's teammates touched him on the shoulder as the stretcher went by like a part of some funeral procession.

A little while later, the announcement came: compound fracture of the right leg (tibia and fibula) for Theismann, who will be in a cast for three months.

Joe Theismann will be forever linked with Lawrence Taylor. "Lawrence Taylor changed my life," Theismann said. "He changed a lot of people's lives. I asked him once: 'LT, did it change you?' He said it proved that no matter how great you are in this game, it can be over in an instant."

Taylor said the incident "made me realize this game is a dangerous game. I know when I saw the look on his face and I saw the injury itself, it made me a little scared—it slaps you in the face. Now, nearly 14 years later, the image of Taylor standing over Theismann and frantically waving for trainers to come on the field is still an eerie one.

Little-known fact: The next morning, Taylor called Theismann in the hospital. Theismann told Taylor he broke both bones in his leg. Theismann laughed when recalling LT's response. "Joe, you got to understand," he said. "I just don't do things halfway."

—Gary Myers, August 1, 1999

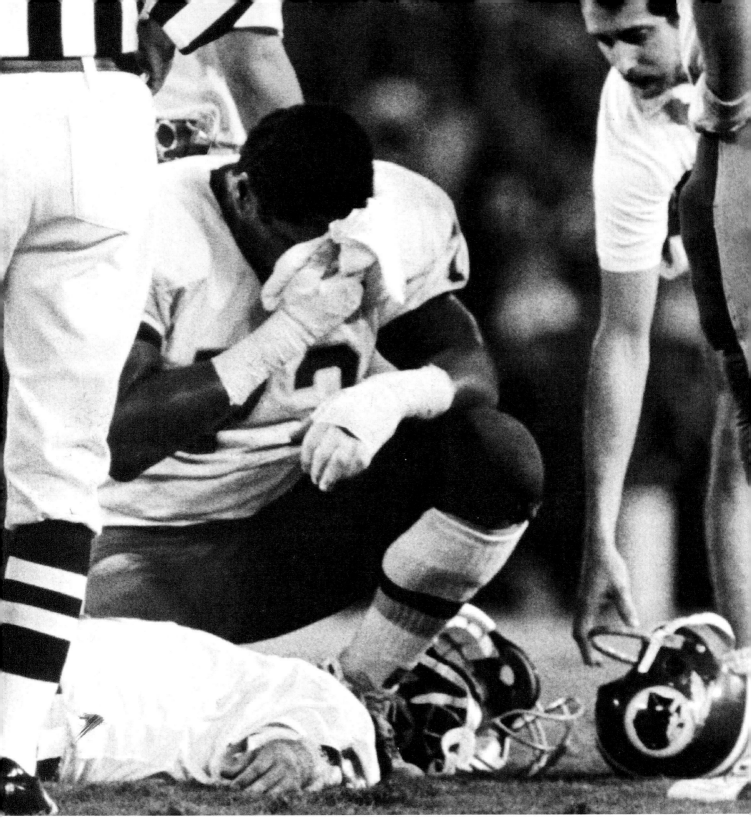

JOE THEISMANN IS ATTENDED TO BY PLAYERS AND OFFICIALS AFTER THE FATEFUL SACK BY LAWRENCE TAYLOR. THE DAY AFTER THE TAYLOR-THEISMANN COLLISION, MIKE LUPICA OF THE DAILY NEWS WROTE: "IT WAS THE SORT OF HIT THAT QUARTERBACKS FEAR, THE WAY JOCKEYS FEAR THE FALL IN TRAFFIC AND THE HITTERS FEAR THE BASEBALL BEHIND THE EAR. IT IS THE SORT OF HIT THAT ENDS A SEASON, AND MAYBE A CAREER." (HARRY HAMBURG, DAILY NEWS)

GIANTS RUSH IN

Gain Playoffs on Morris' 202 Yards

BY BILL VERIGAN   DECEMBER 22, 1985

No barroom vigils are required. No excruciating waits by the television set are necessary. The Giants didn't back into the playoffs this time. They rode in on record-shattering Joe Morris' vapor trail yesterday with a 28-10 victory over the Steelers.

This game was a convincer for Shoeless Joe and the Giants. Contrary to what their detractors have said, the Giants proved they belonged in the playoffs. They proved they can win an important game when it's absolutely necessary.

Morris has been Mr. December.

You know what he did in December? In four games, he gained 542 yards and scored 10 touchdowns.

Bill Parcells said Mr. December has become better with each passing month. Morris was never better than yesterday, carrying 36 times (he never carried more than 31 times, even at Syracuse), gaining 202 yards (only 16 shy of Gene Roberts' club record set on Nov. 12, 1950, vs. the Chicago Cardinals) and scoring three touchdowns.

He got his first 100-yard game this season on Oct. 27. Now he has one 200-yard game and five other 100-yard efforts. Three times during December he scored three TDs. It has been an amazing month.

It might have been better yesterday, except for penalties that cost him 30 yards, and a curious goal-line ruling that denied him a fourth touchdown.

"Awww, he did all right," deadpanned Lawrence Taylor, adding quickly: "I'll tell ya, I'm glad it was a nationally televised game. A lot of people wondered why he made the Pro Bowl. Now they know why he made the Pro Bowl."

JOE MORRIS HAS BEEN CALLED "MR. DECEMBER" BECAUSE OF HIS ABIL-
ITY TO COME THROUGH FOR THE GIANTS DURING THE PLAYOFFS. (DAILY
NEWS)

PARCELLS MOLDED SUPER GIANTS

BY MIKE LUPICA   JANUARY 24, 1987

This is not George Young's team. It is not the quarterback's team. It is not Lawrence Taylor's team, which is why Taylor's snarls were the only ones to be heard this week. It is Parcells' team. Parcells has stamped this team with his own toughness, his own modesty, and his own ability to take a step back every so often and remember that football—and this vulgar pageant—is supposed to be fun.

"You gotta be able to laugh," Parcells said yesterday. "In this business if you don't laugh, you go crazy."

He tries to make it out to be simple. "If you win," he likes to say, "they let you stay." It's his version of "Just win, baby." He talks about luck and the right personnel and being able to instruct the personnel the right way. But there is more to it with Parcells. Somehow, he has gotten it across to these Giants that their best support system is him. He is one of them when he has to be.

He quietly cleaned up what he perceived to be a drug problem on the Giants. He was there last summer when Taylor needed him. I do not believe his relationship with Young is something from the Harlequin Romance series, but never in public has Parcells said a contrary word. Parcells is not an upstairs guy at Giants Stadium, anyway. He is downstairs all the way.

OPPOSITE: LAWRENCE TAYLOR AND COACH BILL PARCELLS DISCUSS DEFENSIVE STRATEGY AT TRAINING CAMP. WITH TAYLOR'S TERRORIZING DEFENSE LEADING THE CHARGE, PARCELLS COACHED THE GIANTS TO SUPER BOWL WINS IN 1987 AND 1991. (WILLIAM LAFORCE, DAILY NEWS)

SUPER 2ND HALF LIFTS GIANTS TO NFL TITLE

BY BILL VERIGAN   JANUARY 26, 1987

After 30 seasons without an NFL title and the stigma of five consecutive losses in NFL championships, the Giants turned destiny into reality with sheer guts and Phil Simms in the second half yesterday to defeat the Broncos in Super Bowl XXI, 39-20.

The Giants and Broncos differed on the turning point.

The Broncos said they lost when they had the Giants down in the first half, and Rich Karlis blew two field goals and the officials blew a replay call.

The Giants said they won when they first gambled on a fake punt on fourth-and-one on the first series of the second half and got the first down, and then completed a 44-yard flea-flicker pass from Simms to Phil McConkey in the third quarter. The Broncos gained two yards in that quarter, while the Giants scored 17 points.

Quite honestly, there were many big plays. And Simms made a majority of them.

"This game should dispel any myths that are lingering about Phil Simms," said Giants' coach Bill Parcells. "I don't think a quarterback had a performance like that in any game this season."

The announcement with 2:03 left that Simms was the game's MVP was an anticlimax after such a performance. He was a unanimous selection, and teammates hugged him, then Bart Oates and Brad Benson doused him with Gatorade. He received that honor before Parcells.

And then there were tears in the eyes of the Giant faithful as Jim Burt charged around the field with his son on his shoulders, then climbed into the stands again to hug and high-five the fans.

There was dancing, with Pepper Johnson and William Roberts leading a conga line around the field.

And there was silence as Wellington Mara, the 70-year-old co-owner of the team, accepted the Super Bowl trophy named for Vince Lombardi.

PHIL MCCONKEY IS HOISTED BY MARK BAVARO AFTER SCORING A TOUCHDOWN IN SUPER BOWL XXI. (KEITH TORRIE, DAILY NEWS)

SIMMS MARCHES INTO HISTORY

BY MIKE LUPICA   JANUARY 26, 1987

They held the parade in Pasadena. It was a Rose Bowl Parade with Giants. The Grand Marshal was a quarterback named Phil Simms.

In the biggest game of his life, in Super Bowl XXI, Phil Simms tried to throw the football equivalent of a perfect game. Simms was 22 for 25, 268 yards, 3 touchdowns.

In the second half, he was 10 for 10, 165 yards, 2 touchdowns. The Giants won, 39-20. It was their first National Football League championship since 1956.

Simms did more than just win the game's MVP award. Simms nearly went back to 1956, too. Simms nearly Don Larsen-ed the Denver Broncos. The quarterback from little Moorehead State gave the Broncos a very bad case of little-town Blues.

All his career, Phil Simms has heard about who he was not. He was not Charlie Conerly, and he was not Y.A. Tittle; in the minds of Giants fans, he was not Fran Tarkenton.

So, he went out and tried to throw a perfect game. To let everyone who ever doubted him know this: In the 213 postseason games in NFL history, no quarterback was ever Phil Simms. No one ever threw for an 88% completion average. Not Conerly or Tittle. Not Unitas or Starr or Bradshaw or Montana.

It was a performance that was an eloquent statement about his skill, his toughness, his patience. It was a performance to drown out all the boos he has heard as the Giants' quarterback. He kept throwing completion after completion. He kept leading the parade. This was something loud. Something unforgettable.

In the end, the Broncos had a problem in Super Bowl XXI: John Elway was not Phil Simms. As far as Super Bowl quarterbacks go, it means Elway can join the club.

Simms was 22 for 25. Simms was 268 yards. Simms was three touchdowns. It was some parade.

PHIL SIMMS CELEBRATES AFTER THROWING ONE OF HIS THREE TOUCH-
DOWN PASSES TO LEAD THE GIANTS OVER THE DENVER BRONCOS, 39-
20, IN SUPER BOWL XXI. (DAILY NEWS)

GIANT 'D' PHILS VOID

BY BILL VERIGAN   NOVEMBER 28, 1988

With Phil Simms cheering on the sideline after being placed on the inactive list just an hour before the game, Paul McFadden kicked a 35-yard field goal with 21 seconds remaining last night for an unbelievable 13-12 Giants' victory over the favored New Orleans Saints.

Without Simms, the Giants used two quarterbacks—Jeff Hostetler and Jeff Rutledge—but they needed one of the greatest defensive efforts that a Giant team has ever put together to squeeze out the victory.

No one could deny the greatness of the Giant 'D', which also played hurt. Lawrence Taylor could barely get up after several plays, and Carl Banks was inactive along with Simms. The Giants' victory was heart stopping, especially for the defense, which did not allow a touchdown.

"I never saw the defense play better than that," said 35-year-old George Martin, "and I've been around a year or two."

TAYLOR MADE FOR FAME

Lawrence Taylor and Bill Parcells say the game that stands out in Taylor's Hall of Fame career was in New Orleans in 1988, when Taylor dominated with 10 tackles, three sacks, and two forced fumbles—despite playing with a painful torn pectoral muscle. Parcells called it LT's "greatest moment."

After the game, Parcells said, "I went up to him and got him alone in the trainer's room. I put my forehead on his forehead and said, 'You were great tonight,' and he said, 'I don't know how I did it.' But I knew. He was Lawrence Taylor." A player like Taylor comes along only once for a coach. "You find me another one and I might coach another 10 or 15 years," Parcells said.

—Gary Myers, August 1, 1999

LAWRENCE TAYLOR REVOLUTIONIZED NFL DEFENSES AND HELPED RE-
STORE THE GIANTS' PROUD TRADITION OF WINNING. "IT'S HARD TO QUAN-
TIFY WHAT HE DID FOR US," GIANTS OWNER WELLINGTON MARA SAID. "HE
WAS OUR PHYSICAL AND SPIRITUAL LEADER, WITHOUT ANY QUESTION."
(DAILY NEWS)

SUPER TROOPERS MARCH TO CROWN

BY BARRY MEISEL   JANUARY 28, 1991

The Giants won the Super Bowl last night on their terms. They forced the Buffalo Bills to work at their deliberate pace, at their methodical tempo, in front of a lively Tampa Stadium crowd of 73,813 that vocally was weighted in favor of the NFC champions in blue.

Sure, the Bills' offense hurried by not huddling. Yes, Jim Kelly passed and Thurman Thomas ran, and Andre Reed caught crossing patterns. But the Giants didn't panic when they fell behind by nine midway through the second quarter.

They slowed the Bills by hogging the ball for more than 40 minutes. Their defense stiffened in the 20 minutes it was on the field. Their special teams dominated and ultimately decided the game.

And so four years and two days after their first Super Bowl triumph, they did it again.

Bill Parcells' well-balanced mix of veterans, kids, castoffs, and substitutes captured the closest and most thrilling Super Bowl in history, 20-19. Four years and two days ago, Pepper Johnson and William Roberts danced deliriously on the Rose Bowl turf after the Giants beat the Broncos. Last night, Johnson and Roberts replayed that midfield scene with two new dance partners, Myron Guyton and Lee Rouson.

And Steve DeOssie caught it all on the video camera he used to record Scott Norwood's 47-yard miss of a game-winning field goal.

Wellington Mara and his nephew, Tim Mara, accepted their second Vince Lombardi Trophy in five years—the NFC's seventh straight—because seven minutes after Matt Bahr's 21-yard field goal gave the Giants their slim lead, Norwood lined up for his attempt from the right hash mark with eight seconds remaining and kicked it wide of the right upright with four seconds left.

(GERALD HERBERT, DAILY NEWS)

(AP/WIDE WORLD PHOTOS)

THE GIANTS' PRAYERS (TOP) WERE ANSWERED WHEN BUFFALO KICKER SCOTT NORWOOD MISSED THE GAME-WINNING FIELD GOAL (CENTER). THE TEAM CELEBRATED BY DOUSING COACH BILL PARCELLS (LEFT).

(KEITH TORRIE, DAILY NEWS)

147

GIANTS FIND THIS ENDING OH, SO SWEET

BY GARY MYERS   JANUARY 28, 1991

Bill Parcells and Lawrence Taylor ran off the field arm-in-arm to the sounds of Frank Sinatra's "New York, New York," blasting on the stadium speakers. Then LT leaned over and gave Parcells a big wet one on the cheek.

The Giants couldn't control their emotions last night like they controlled those no-huddle Bills. On his way out of the locker room and into the night, Parcells was greeted by about 200 Giants fans lined behind a barricade. They were screaming for him, and Parcells gave them that toothy Super Bowl championship smile.

"It just doesn't get any better than this," Parcells said. "It's better than anything I know. I don't know why God chose to bless Bill Parcells, but he did. The last two weeks God has been playing for us."

Two weeks in a row of this stuff is too much. Last week, the Giants prayed and Matt Bahr hit a 42-yard field goal at the buzzer to beat San Francisco. The prayer group reconvened with eight seconds remaining last night and Scott Norwood about to attempt a 47-yard field goal. They willed this one wide to the right.

In the locker room after the 20-19 victory, which was simply the best of the XXV Super Bowls played, it didn't take long for the Giants to put on the blue Super Bowl caps and T-shirts. Everson Walls had to walk away from his podium in the interview room when he started crying. And in what could be a Super Bowl first, Steve DeOssie took his video camera out of a bag on the sidelines and recorded Norwood's miss.

The Giants had played a magnificent game. No team has ever shown more heart. "Individuals don't win football games. Teams do," Walls said. "And this is the best team collectively that I've seen in a long time."

GIANTS LEONARD MARSHALL AND PEPPER JOHNSON CELEBRATE THE SACK OF BUFFALO QUARTERBACK JIM KELLY IN THE SECOND QUARTER OF SUPER BOWL XXV. (GERALD HERBERT, DAILY NEWS)

REEVES IS
COACH OF THE YEAR

BY HANK GOLA   JANUARY 7, 1994

Dan Reeves, who guided the Giants out of the despair of the last two years and back into the playoffs after being fired in Denver, has blown away the field for NFL Coach of the Year.

Reeves yesterday received 68 of 81 votes cast by the Associated Press' national panel of sportswriters and sportscasters. Oilers coach Jack Pardee got six votes. Don Shula, Dave Wannstedt, and Jimmy Johnson got two each, and Bill Parcells, the last Giant to win the award, got one vote for turning around the Patriots.

"This is an accumulation of a lot of things," Reeves said yesterday. "It's not me coming in here and all of a sudden they're successful because of me. It's a combination of a lot of people working together to do a job."

Reeves brought discipline back to a Giants team that had lost it in the chaotic reign of Ray Handley. Reeves ended the quarterback controversy by settling on Phil Simms and reshaped the team by making tough player cuts. Almost every decision he made turned out for the best, and the momentum built into an 11-5 season, far above even his own expectations.

Reeves, who turns 50 this month, said again he was hurt when he was fired in Denver. "I really didn't think that was ever going to happen to me but it did," he said. "It happened to coach (Tom) Landry and it can happen to anybody in any phase of life.

"But I do know that I've been in this game for 29 years and I've been a winner most all of those years, so I know what it takes. I know you've got to have a team attitude, and that's what I've always stressed."

Reeves is the third Giant coach to win the award, the second to do so in his first season. Before Parcells in 1986, Allie Sherman was Coach of the Year in his first two years as Giant coach, 1961 and 1962.

ALTHOUGH DAN REEVES' COACHING TENURE WITH THE GIANTS (1993-96) WAS TUMULTUOUS AT TIMES, IT INCLUDED ONE OF THE MOST DRAMATIC TURNAROUNDS IN GIANTS HISTORY. TAKING OVER A 6-10 TEAM, REEVES LED THE 1993 GIANTS TO AN 11-5 RECORD AND A PLAYOFF VICTORY OVER THE MINNESOTA VIKINGS, EARNING HIMSELF COACH OF THE YEAR HONORS. (DAILY NEWS)

RODNEY'S IN FOR LONG RUN

BY MIKE LUPICA   JANUARY 10, 1994

Doug Riesenberg went outside to make a block and Howard Cross killed somebody inside and Rodney Hampton cut back and suddenly Hampton had some room on the right sideline. Carlos Jenkins of the Vikings seemed to have Hampton in his sights, but Rodney brushed him off with his left hand and kept going. Now Hampton was in the clear on the second Sunday in January. Now Rodney Hampton was running hard down the right sideline toward a destination that would have seemed impossible in September. He was running toward Candlestick Park.

Hampton got to the Vikings 20. Chris Calloway, who is 5-10, was in front of him blocking Vencie Glenn of the Vikings. In these moments at Giants Stadium, Calloway was as big as Jumbo Elliott. Glenn could not get to Rodney Hampton. The touchdown run would be 51 yards. It is Hampton's longest run from scrimmage all season. It is the longest postseason run from scrimmage in Giants history. It is only the biggest play of this remarkable Giants season.

"The playoffs are a good time to pop one," Hampton said. He ended up with 161 yards on 33 carries. He is as important to the Giants as Emmitt Smith is to the Cowboys. And he is as dangerous as a pass play. If Hampton breaks this kind of play last week against the Cowboys, no one gets worked up over Dan Reeves' play-calling. The whole tri-state area sleeps much better.

The cheers were for all the Sundays, and for next Saturday, at Candlestick Park. Wind and fortune and finally the strong legs of Rodney Hampton carry an improbable Giants season all the way back there.

OPPOSITE: DRAFTED IN 1990, RODNEY HAMPTON WENT ON TO HAVE AN ILLUSTRIOUS RUSHING CAREER. HE IS THE ONLY GIANT BACK TO RUSH FOR MORE THAN 1,000 YARDS IN FIVE CONSECUTIVE SEASONS, AND HE TOPS THE GIANTS' LIST FOR YARDS GAINED IN A CAREER WITH 6,897. (KEITH TORRIE, DAILY NEWS)

LINE CLEARS LANE FOR HAMPTON EXPRESS

BY HANK GOLA   SEPTEMBER 25, 1995

Rodney Hampton has carried the ball more times than any other Giants running back. Not many of those 1,330 attempts went as smoothly as the 33 he had yesterday against the hapless Saints.

With Hampton rolling for 149 yards and a club-record four TDs and understudy Tyrone Wheatley adding 54 yards and his first NFL score, the Giants followed an age-old formula to their first victory.

"Whenever the line's excited and jumping around, picking me off the ground, I know something big is going to happen," Hampton said. "Those guys love blocking and it showed."

"It's terrific," said tackle Jumbo Elliott, one of Hampton's main escorts. "Rodney gets in that groove and starts to feel it, it seems like everything else clicks a little smoother."

Things clicked so well against the NFL's worst defense that the Giants, who previously scored one offensive touchdown, had their biggest point output since 1986. Hampton never stopped churning as he passed Joe Morris' career mark for carries and had the first four-touchdown rushing day in team history.

He scored from one, five, two, and three yards out and averaged 4.5 yards. Wheatley also had 54 yards on 10 carries and pulverized cornerback Jimmy Spencer on his way to the end zone.

"Hampton's a great back," said Saints middle linebacker Richard Harvey. "He picked and chose his holes well. He got up in there for a big man. He stutter-stepped and turned on the speed and got outside and did what he had to do."

Rodney Hampton's GIANT Records

#1   Giants' all-time rushing yards (6,897)

#1   Most points in a game (24, tied with two others)

#3   Most touchdowns in a season (14, tied with several others)

#1   Most rushing touchdowns in a game (4)

#1   Most Career rushing attempts (1,824)

#2   Most rushing attempts in a season (327)

#2   Most Rushing attempts in a game (41)

#3   Most Rushing yards in a season (1,182)

#4   Most Rushing yards in a game (187)

#2   Most games with 100 yards or more rushing (17)

#1   Most rushing touchdowns in a career (49)

#2   Most Rushing touchdowns in a season
(14, tied with two others)

GIANTS PEAKING AT PERFECT TIME, SEZ FASSEL

Finish Undefeated in NFC East

BY LUKE CYPHERS   DECEMBER 23, 1997

Jim Fassel won't even look at the tape of the Giants' 20-7 drubbing of Dallas, so he can't say for certain. But the Giants' head coach suspects his team is now playing its best football all year, just in time for the playoffs.

"I hope we're peaking, because we need it right now," said Fassel, the rookie coach whose young NFC East champions will host the Vikings Saturday in a first-round playoff game. "But I think maybe we are."

Fassel recalled yesterday that going into the crucial final three games of the season—against Philadelphia on the road, Washington at home, and at Dallas—he and his staff discussed the importance of making a mark in those games and establishing themselves as a factor in the playoffs.

With the postseason in doubt just three weeks ago, the Giants definitely made their mark, sweeping all three games by a combined score of 81-38 to finish the season at 10-5-1, 7-0-1 in the division. No team in NFC East history had gone through the division without a loss until these Giants.

"We may have put together our three best games back-to-back right in a row," Fassel said. "We're playing right now with a lot of confidence, a lot of aggressiveness."

As "perfect" as the 1997 Giants were in the NFC East, their season ended earlier than expected with a shocking playoff loss to the Minnesota Vikings, 23-22, at Giants Stadium.

TAYLOR INDUCTED INTO HALL OF FAME

BY MIKE LUPICA   AUGUST 8, 1999

They would do anything to stop him—maybe about half of it legal in football—once everybody could see how good Lawrence Taylor really was.

They would block him with a tight end, a running back, a tackle, even a guard sometimes, making it four against one. It still wasn't a fair fight, even when some of those guys would try to trip him on the way by.

The 49ers were one of the first to use a guard, mostly because they were afraid Taylor was going to break Joe Montana in half. Taylor got to Montana anyway. He got to everybody. You couldn't stop him.

Now he makes it to the Hall of Fame in Canton, Ohio. He tried to stop himself on the way there, plenty of times. He kept trying to get in his own way, put himself and his demons between his talent and the Hall, which he only deserves as much as anyone who ever played.

In so many ways, he was our Mantle in football, because of the thrilling way he played the game, because of his excesses. Taylor's body was just stronger. On defense in football, he was as big as life as Babe Ruth. He was that much ahead of the field. Ruth was another who could stay up all night and then own the next day. Great players, bad boys.

Parcells was the Giants' defensive coordinator under head coach Ray Perkins when Taylor arrived from North Carolina in the summer of 1981. Parcells had a lot of good linebackers, and his plan was to ease the kid into the lineup behind them, maybe have him playing regularly by the middle of the '81 season.

The plan lasted exactly one week.

"I gotta get this kid into the game," Parcells told Perkins.

He would have 132 1/2 quarterback sacks by the end of his career and more than 1,000 tackles, and would force 33 fumbles. You never needed a program, not for one minute, not for the greatest football player of them all.

AP/WIDE WORLD

LAWRENCE TAYLOR'S HALL OF FAME STATS:

10 STRAIGHT PRO BOWL SELECTIONS (1981-9

10 STRAIGHT ALL-NFL SELECTIONS (1981-9

1981 NFL DEFENSIVE ROOKIE OF THE YEA

1981, '82, '86 NFL DEFENSIVE PLAYER OF THE

1986 NFL MVP (PRO FOOTBALL WRITERS A

ALL-NFL TEAM OF THE 1980S (HALL OF FAME

#1 GIANTS ALL-TIME SACK LEADER (132

#1 GIANTS SACK LEADER IN A SEASON (

*DOES NOT INCLUDE 9.5 SACKS IN 1981, BEFORE SACKS WERE